PRAISE FOR
TO GOD AND MY COUNTRY

"This book will cause some deep soul searching and challenge your heart to realize what is important in life. Once you read it, you will make the hard choices and know the real meaning of what is easy and wrong or hard and right".
– **Ron Wallace**, Former President of UPS International & Author of *Leadership Lessons from a UPS Driver*

"We revere our childhood as a special point in time which provides us with fond memories of youthfulness and new experiences. Regrettably, we place these memories aside from adulthood as if they were meant for old shoebox to be set aside in a closet and forgotten. In *To God and My Country,* Matt Kunz has pulled off the rarest of feats because he never put away his shoebox. Matt takes us on an incredible journey vividly painting the picture of how his experiences in scouting provided him with the principles of leadership, the value of mentoring, and how his wisdom and faith in God shaped his character. Because of scouting, today, Matt is a successful coach, mentor, motivational speaker, and an elected official who inspires those around him to open their own shoeboxes!"
– **George Gordon**, Executive Officer / PIO, City of Alpharetta Department of Public Safety

"Any young person who is trying to discern their dream and follow it needs to read *To God and My Country*. I'm honored to recommend this book!"
– **Becky Wynn**, former Roswell City Councilwoman

"No matter your age, *To God and My Country* presents a dynamic of leadership rarely offered by other authors. Yes, you'll acquire the knowledge of *how* to lead. However, you'll also acquire the wisdom of *why* leadership challenges exist in the first place."
– **Jerry Orlans**, Roswell City Councilman, Licensed Insurance Counselor / Consultant, RBC Benefits, Inc. / BIS Benefits

"To God and My Country is a testimonial that the Boy Scouts of America holds the honor of being the premier youth organization for moral leadership training in the U.S.A. Kunz joins the legions of many of American leaders who have hiked the trail to Eagle. *To God and My Country* should be required reading for boys of scouting age and be an appendix to the Scout Handbook."
– **W. C. Lusk**, Patriot

"To *God and My Country* reflects the importance of life's merit badges necessary to build skills which are required to be a good leader. As I read this book, I reflected on my own Eagle Scout Badge and how important the skills learned as a teenager formed a solid foundation for my career and life. The chapters are entertaining as they provide great life learning moments."
– **Mark Wyssbrod**, CPA, Eagle Scout, 2015 Georgia Society of CPAs Public Service Aware, 2013 Small Business Person of the Year for the Greater North Fulton Chamber of Commerce.

"To God and My Country is a great follow-up to *Triumph!* Both books have many life lessons that are applicable to all of us. Listen and remember, always be prepared, and soar with eagles. Matt Kunz is a talented young author. I cannot wait for his next book!"
– **Robert M. Rosner**, CLU

To God

and

My Country

By:

Matt Kunz

Cover Design by Greg Simanson
Edited by Carolyn Ridder Aspenson
Proofread by Matt Higbee
Book Managed by Katie Wacek

Print ISBN 978-0-9976298-2-8
EPub ISBN 978-0-9976298-3-5

Library of Congress Control Number
2016911406

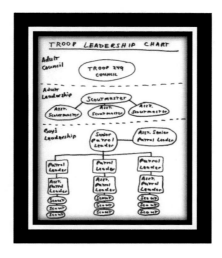

To all leaders and adventurers everywhere,
but especially to the boys of Troop 249.
May every one of you soar like an Eagle!

Dear Bill,

Always strive to

soar like an Eagle!

Your Friend,

Mark King

Table of Contents

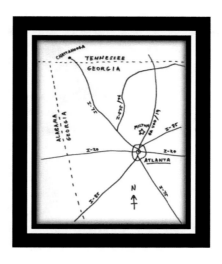

INTRODUCTION

THE RAIN CAME DOWN IN BUCKETS, but that did not stop my wife from fervently waving our sign at all the cars turning into the Milton High School Football game. When she encouraged me to run for office, I knew it would be tough on her, and that is what scared me more than anything. Still, there she was, standing brave and strong, her curly hair drenched from the downpour, and holding a campaign sign with my name on it. She was truly amazing.

Until then, the heated campaign became the discussion amongst residents at their dinner tables, and it caught the attention of State legislatures as they worked on regional issues. I was an unknown, and many wondered who I was when I entered my name in the hat to run for City Council. In the beginning, few on our team held hope for a win. Yet, that night several months later, with my wife, some friends, and about fifteen enthusiastic teenagers waving our signs, I knew we had turned the corner. Our opponent and her volunteers had been at that very same corner, but I guess the rain was too much for them as they had given up and left, their commitment to the election dampened by the downpour. As the people in the cars waved at us, I knew that in a few weeks change would happen in our city, and with that would come a new course of leadership.

Moments like these do not come accidentally. Life often brings lessons our way at an early age, and we have only to accept them for what they are, understand them, learn from them, and apply them in the future. As I recalled our campaign, and all the stories of friends and foes and of heroes and villains, I realized many of those stories were actually repeats of experiences I had at an earlier age. True, the setting and the cast of characters were different, but the lessons were the same. I came to understand that wisdom is not age specific. Neither has human nature changed.

Thus, I wanted to share these lessons through those stories from that earlier age, which was my time in Troop 249 of the Boy Scouts of America. As you read these stories, I hope to take you to a simpler time, a time with no cell phones and no internet, but one in which the world, in all its nature and power, was just as fierce as it is today.

However, through it all, I hope you come to believe that we can overcome and appreciate the world when we make good choices and learn to stick together. Then, in the end, we realize how strong we can be when we find we are able spread our wings and fly!

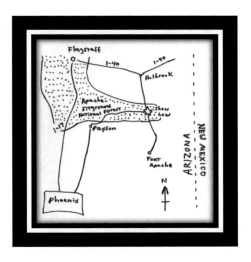

CHAPTER 1
FAIRNESS

ASLIGHT CHILL EDGED ITS WAY into the evening air. Green leaves began to turn into their fall shades of red and orange. With the summer now over, and the school year already begun, my parents enlisted me in a Cub Scout troop to which a friend of mine belonged. I was thrilled. The shirts were a dark shade of blue, my favorite color. Many of the patches came in a bright gold color, easy to see displayed on the shirt's chest pocket of a dedicated Cub Scout. There were so many different patches, but each of them had their own special meaning. Most importantly, the patches were not free. A Cub Scout could not get a patch for just any reason. To have the privilege to wear a patch, he had to earn it, and that appealed to me. Earning a badge was an honor, and a scout had to achieve a mission in order to wear his badge. I was all for it.

I breathed in the fall mountain air as I took my seat on the front porch patio with my new pack. In front of me, our Cub Master said he had some news for us. He told us that a local business group was going to invite us for a Halloween party. It was quite an honor, as that particular Elks Lodge was made up of community leaders and business owners. There would be food and cake for us, and there would be a competition, too.

Our Cub Master said, "The Elks Lodge decided to have a contest among you. The theme is Halloween, and they suggested that each of you make a paper mache mask. I don't care what kind of mask you make, but make it something scary."

"How about I make one of my sister!" shouted a boy. This caused a laugh, but the Cub Master calmed us down and continued.

"Now, you should all know that this will be a contest, and the Elks Lodge members are going to award first and second prizes to the best and scariest masks. So, you're going to want to do a good job to see who will win," he continued. He would spend the next few minutes teaching us how to put together a mask.

Creating the masks was a long process, and one we could not complete in a single meeting. In fact, we began in September because it would take us at least three weeks to complete it with a fourth week to allow for some finishing touches. We had to first develop our concept during week one. During week two, we pasted the newspaper in the shape we wanted and, because the mask had to dry, we waited a third week to paint it. By week four, we had to be done.

For a seven year old, this was a big deal and I was very excited about the competition. I just knew I was going to win. My mask evolved into a gruesome grey ghost mask with a creepy mouth and eyes. I scrutinized the other masks and felt confident that mine would win first place. Another Scout next to me was putting a mask together that looked like a deranged green alien and I believed that it would take second. On my left was a crazed werewolf mask, but I thought it looked more like an otter. That one, I thought, had no chance. When week four finished, I placed my grey ghost carefully in the box with all the others. I gazed up at the Cub Master, pride running through my veins, and said to him, "Be careful with it. It's a winner." He paused, smiled gently, and shut the box.

After what seemed like a lifetime, the big day came. I thought I needed to look sharp for the moment when I would receive my prize. As I was putting my uniform on, I examined how I looked in the mirror. I had to be sure I had room to hold the first prize ribbon. "Maybe they would pin it on me," I thought. "Or, if I have to carry it around, that would be ok, too."

My parents and I drove to the ceremony, and I was in awe once we walked into the lodge. There they were, all of our masks hung along the inside wall for everyone to see. Mine hung in its ghostly splendor. For a brief second I imagined a big blue ribbon hanging next to it.

During the party, everyone passed the time by snacking on food and cake, while the Scouts eagerly anticipated the beginning of the competition. Finally, the moment arrived. It was time to judge. The Elks Lodge president stood, gathered everybody around, and said a few words. Excited and nervous, I wanted him to stop wasting time and get to the point. Then he said something that caught my attention. "Now, judging tonight, we have our newest member," and he pointed at my father. "We're very glad to have him, and he's been gracious to help us with this contest," he said.

"Wait…what!?" I gasped! I knew my father, and frankly, I was not surprised they selected him to be the judge. He had not only been a professional athlete, but the lodge members also admired him for his wit, intelligence, and personality. He was always someone who did the right thing, and that gave me a bad feeling that he would not pick my ghost simply because I was his son. I looked worriedly up at my mother and whispered, "Mom, Dad's not going to pick me," whereas she quickly reminded me not to interrupt.

My eyes began to water and my throat tightened. "This is not fair!" I thought. What chance would I have in a contest if my father were the judge? He would not want to show favoritism by picking my mask, even if it was the best. I agreed with the sentiment, but it still upset me. His involvement automatically excluded me from the competition. A part of me hoped he'd be so overcome by the majesty of my grey ghost that I was getting all worked up for nothing. As my dad got up to say a few words, he said, "And the winner is…" and I could not believe my ears.

"Not the deranged alien!" I thought. "This isn't right!" Sure enough, a lodge member removed the deranged green alien from the wall, gave it to my competitor, and handed him a blue ribbon. "Maybe Second Prize…?" I hoped, and they brought down the otter-looking werewolf. I was stunned. "You've got to be kidding me!" I thought, and I tugged at my mom's arm. Finally, I said, "Mom, this isn't right!" and as tears welled up I began to become very visibly upset.

After the ceremony ended, my father walked over to me and said, "Now, Son, you know I couldn't pick your mask because you were my son. That wouldn't look right to everyone else."

"I know," I said wiping tears from my eyes. "But I worked so hard on that mask. Because you were the judge, I didn't even have a chance. I don't understand why *you* had to be the judge in the first place."

Dad sighed and did not say anything. He stood up, and I looked to my left at my fellow cub scout holding the deranged alien with the blue ribbon. I did not want to understand why they asked my father to be the judge, but deep inside I knew the reason. Dad was a celebrity in a small town, and I knew it was an honor for them to ask him. However, my father found himself in a tough spot, one that put me at a disadvantage. If my father had voted for me, both he and I would have turned friends into enemies. He sacrificed my mask so that would not happen. In the grand scheme of things, his relationships with the members of the Elks Lodge were far more important than my paper mache mask. Still, at seven years old, I was not willing to understand. The way I saw it, my mask and the competition were all that mattered. My father had a right to his opinion, and if he felt the deranged alien was truly the best, then fine.

Thus, I learned from that mask competition, at the age of seven, how politics enters into so many areas of competition. It is so important for the system to be fair and impartial, yet that is difficult to do when you consider the various relationships entangled amongst each other.

It is the responsibility of our leaders in both business and politics to search for truth in order to overcome the pulls and pushes of our relationships. If truth can be determined, then our leaders must defend that truth. However, if only an opinion is required, our leaders should make that opinion only after letting everyone have a chance at voicing theirs. The leader's opinion may or may not change, but at the very least all points should be considered. Finally, I learned, that night as my father showed me, that sometimes it is better to lose a battle and walk away than to lose the war. Our leaders need to know which battles to choose, and from which to walk away.

That night, as we left the building, I held my grey ghost in my hand, trophy-less. I silently dropped my ghost into a trashcan, a disappearing apparition never seen again.

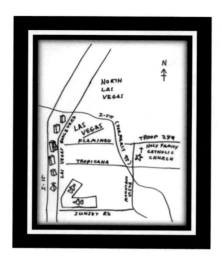

CHAPTER 2
CHOOSING

THE NEXT YEAR, my father's business moved us away from the small town to the growing city of Las Vegas. Because of the change, I did not stay in the Cub Scouts. Instead, I spent my time on school and homework, and not much else. Unfortunately, that lack of activity caused me to put on some weight. Concerned that I was not getting enough exercise, my parents signed me up for soccer, and that's where I met my friend, Richie.

Richie and I were both big kids from Catholic families with similar interests. Running, however, was not one of those interests. Our coaches stuck Richie and me in the back to defend the goal with our far more athletic goalie. We were told to charge if our opponent brought the ball up the field. If we happened to run someone over along the way, our coach told us to be sure we ran over someone from the other team. Also, make sure we kicked the ball towards the other goal when doing so. This would continue for years.

Somewhere along the way, I thought of joining the Boy Scouts. At eleven, I was too old for Cub Scouts, and I would be getting a late start at the Boy Scouts, but that did not matter. I just knew that my local church had one so I decided to talk with them.

I expressed interest in joining a troop to my mother, and I called someone to find out the day and time that our church troop met. We put the appointed time on the calendar. My excitement and anticipation grew as my first troop meeting drew closer.

When the day finally arrived, I could barely contain my excitement. As we pulled into the parking lot, three boys dressed in disheveled Boy Scout uniforms raced to the car next to us, crashing into its trunk with an unpleasant "Bang!" They were playing a game. Their shirts were untucked, their hats were off, and their hair was a mess. The two larger boys held cans and sprayed something into the third boy's hair. He ducked, his arms flailing all over the place. My mother flashed a disapproving look, but didn't say a word. Quickly we walked toward the building.

When we opened the door, I realized that what we had just witnessed outside was only a piece of what was happening inside. Boys raced and darted through the entire building. One boy stood on a table, flinging his arms in the air while shouting triumphantly. Four or five others grabbed and pulled at him, trying to get him to fall. A soccer ball flew across the room and it landed with a smack on another boy's head. Paper soared through the air like arrows and spears in a medieval battle zone. Balls bounced. Kids raced and jumped. My heart raced as we took in the madness. Suddenly a short adult scoutmaster stood before us.

"Hello there!" he said, smiling. "They're a wild bunch, aren't they?" That's when I noticed the boy on the table had lost his battle, only to have his spot stolen by another boy who proclaimed to be

"King!" His proclamation garnered him his own battle against the very same boys who helped him oust the previous king. "We have a lot of fun here," said the scoutmaster. He appeared to me to be a little on edge.

As I looked inside at the chaos I asked, "Is this what it's like every week?"

"Just about," said the scoutmaster. At that moment, a piece of paper hit him in the head. "Oh, boys will be boys," he said.

"We'll just watch for a few minutes, if that's alright with you." I noticed my mother's displeasing tone, and wondered if the man sensed it also.

"You bet. We'd be glad to have you. Just let me know if you have any questions." After he said this, we heard a loud "Crack!" come from the far side of the room. The table that held the king's throne collapsed. The king toppled to the ground, consumed by the mob of boys below who tortured him with pokes, jabs, and prods. "Boys!" the scoutmaster yelled when the table fell. He looked back at us and said, "If you'll excuse me, I'll need to attend to the group over there." Then he went to the scene of the mob amidst the remnants of the broken table.

I looked at my mother and said, "Mom, if this is it, I don't want to do it. This is crazy!" She nodded and asked me if I wanted to leave. I said, "Yes. Let's go." We climbed into our car and left the parking lot without even saying goodbye. Saddened, I turned back to look at the building behind us. There, in the parking lot, those two same boys sprayed whipped cream into the third boy's mouth. I cringed, wondering if the madness behind us would ever end.

...

Shortly thereafter, I found myself in another soccer game. While Richie and I stood on the field, not running, my mother struck up a conversation with Richie's mother. Richie's mother had two young children, and when one of them ran onto the field during a game, she would jump from her folding chair and chase her child off the field. She did not ask the referees to stop the game; she just took action herself. It was instinctual, a desire to keep her child safe, and my mother admired her for that.

During their conversation, my mother mentioned how disappointed she and I were at the Boy Scout troop we had recently visited. Richie's mom, sensing an opportunity, said, "Well, come on over to our troop. We're Troop 249, and you'll find that our scoutmasters really work at instilling a lot of discipline. Many of them are ex-military, so they know how to do that. Richie's already been all the way through Cub Scouts and Webelos with them, and now he's advancing as a Scout. Come and take a look."

When the referee blew the whistle signaling the end of the game, I went to my mother who was standing next to Richie's mom. "Guess what, Matt," she said. "We're going to check out Richie's Boy Scout troop on Wednesday night.

"Ok," I said. I did not know Richie was in the Scouts, but he was a good guy, so I figured it must be better than what we saw last week.

Wednesday night came and my mother and I drove to the meeting, which the troop held inside a trailer outside a Catholic Church. No boys with spray cans ran around the parking lot. Inside there were no mobs dethroning kings. There were boys out there, but they were well behaved.

Richie's mom greeted us, as did his dad, Chuck. He was a jovial guy with a relaxed appearance who seemed genuinely happy to be there. Chuck, an assistant scoutmaster, wore his hat and uniformed shirt, complete with all the patches awarded to a person of that stature. He introduced us to the scoutmaster, Jeff.

Jeff was a large, imposing man. His eyes were fierce. By the looks of them, there were stories behind those eyes. Stories I feared. Stories that came with the, "If I told you, I'd have to kill you," statement attached. I did not want to make him an enemy. That much I knew.

When they led me into the trailer, I noticed that all the chairs were in rows, and faced the front, toward the flags. Each patrol had their own row, with the leaders sitting near the front. When the meeting started, all the boys quietly came and took their seats. Though it was not silent, I felt a definite improvement compared to the chaos we had seen the prior week.

When the program began, they introduced me, and then followed their agenda. That day they planned to instruct the troop on the tying of knots and their use in the field. Midway through the instruction, there was a brief break for some play, but, a few minutes later, we were back tying knots.

Near the end, Chuck came to me with a list. "If you decide to join the troop," he said, "come back next week and have these things memorized. They are the Scout Oath, the Scout Law, and the Scout Motto. Here's the address of a place where you can get your uniform." Pointing at the list he continued, "Learn to tie the square knot, and you'll be on your way to getting your first patch for your shirt. I might even have an extra patch around to give you if you get all these thing checked off." "These guys are serious," I thought.

Finally, he said, "Also, we have a hike this Saturday at Red Rock. Bring some hiking shoes, a water bottle, and a sack lunch. We'll have a good time." I could not believe it. In two hours, they already helped me earn my first patch and invited me to go hiking. "Sign me up!" I said. I committed right then and there to go hiking on Saturday, and I was determined that I was going to get that patch next week.

These two experiences taught me the importance in finding the right organization to join. Just because one group is closer or more convenient does not mean it is the best group for you. Look at the people you admire and respect. Then consider their organizations, as those will be the ones most likely to suit you. However, sometimes they won't. If you get a feeling about a place that just doesn't sit right, there might be a reason for it. Explore your options. Look to the leadership in the organization. Do they actually lead? Do you believe that they want you to grow, or are they just in it for themselves? Will they have the courage to teach you if you do something wrong? Will they take the effort to reward you if you do something right?

As I look back, I know it is important to build a culture that attracts the right people, one that works to develop the members the right way. That responsibility, though, falls directly on those in charge. That Saturday, as I hiked through the washed out rocks of Red Rock Canyon, I had no idea that I would begin to experience what that meant in just a few short days.

The Gator Patrol Flag

CHAPTER 3
LEADERSHIP BY DEFAULT

THE FOLLOWING WEEK, I showed up at the trailer early so I could run through my checklist and make sure I would earn my patch. I had practiced and prepared. Then, when the meeting began, the senior patrol leader announced to the troop that I had officially become a scout.

Several boys sat in their rows, each row designating a specific patrol within the troop. As new members joined the troop, they were assigned to a patrol based on experience. Newer boys typically stayed together, while the older, more experienced boys had a patrol of their own.

The patch on their right shoulder designated patrols. The oldest, most experienced boys sat in their row together. On their right sleeve was a venomous cobra, thus designating it the "Cobra Patrol" of Troop 249.

I looked at my patrol, formed by the scoutmasters over the past week. Because some of the other patrols had grown so large, the troop leadership decided to throw all new members together into a brand new patrol. They hoped we would figure it out as we went along. I looked at my assigned patrol. In our row, there were eight chairs, but only two other boys besides myself. One had only been there a week longer than I had and this was the third boy's first meeting. I took a seat behind the boy with one week more seniority than me.

"What's our patrol mascot?" I asked him.

"I think it's the squirrel," he said.

"Squirrel?" Are you sure?"

"Here's the patch," he said as he pointed to the emblem on his shoulder.

"Did we pick that?" I asked.

He shook his head. "No. They gave it to us."

"Ok. What's your name?"

"Jimmy," he said.

I leaned back in my chair and thought, "Squirrel? Really?" That's when our scoutmaster spoke. "Ok, men. Today, we are going to have elections for senior patrol leader and patrol leaders."

I looked at the front of the room. Standing to Scoutmaster Jeff was his son, Bob. Already grown big and intimidating like his father, he had decided to run for the position of senior patrol leader, the scout position that ran the entire troop, and I recall thinking I'd be surprised if anyone ran against him. It turned out I was right. The adults distributed ballots and pencils to the boys. I looked at my blank sheet of paper. Since Bob was the only one running, I wrote his name with my pencil, folded my ballot, and sent it to the front. The other boys did the same. In a few short minutes, the scoutmasters announced Bob as the winner and he would be our new senior patrol leader.

After a short moment of excitement, the room quieted. Each scout sat in his designated patrol row, waiting for new instructions. Scoutmaster Jeff then said, "Now, we need each of you to circle with your patrols and together decide who your patrol leaders and assistant patrol leaders are going to be. Take a vote if you need to, but we want you all to huddle together and make a decision."

Upon hearing that, the three of us in the Squirrel Patrol huddled together. "Gosh, I'm here two weeks and we're already having elections? I'm just trying to figure out who thought it would be a good idea to call us Squirrels!" I said.

The other two laughed, and we sat, silently staring at each other for a moment or two, no one offering any suggestion for what to do next.

Finally, I chimed in, "Ok. None of us know each other. So how about we do this? Jimmy, you've been here three weeks. Robby's been here one week. I've been here two weeks. So how about Jimmy be the patrol leader, I'll be assistant patrol leader, and Robby, since you're new you can be, oh I don't know, historian, or something like that. Will that work?"

The other two nodded, and we announced our decision to the troop. Shortly thereafter, the meeting ended and I had my first official capacity assistant leadership position. It wasn't much, but I planned to make the most of it.

The following week, a new boy joined the troop, and our scoutmaster had him join our patrol. Jimmy, our new patrol leader, was not there so, as acting assistant patrol leader, I helped organize my two other Squirrel Patrol members. The next week two more boys joined the troop and they sat with us. I waited for the meeting for Jimmy to arrive and begin aligning the boys, but he never showed. I once again took the initiative and organized our small but growing patrol.

16

The Squirrel Patrol gained two more boys in week three, but again, Jimmy was not at the meeting. I sensed a pattern. On the fourth week, after another new member joined our patrol, Jimmy was still absent. I needed help, so I went to Scoutmaster Jeff and said, "Sir, Jimmy hasn't been at our meetings now for four weeks, but he's our patrol leader. Since he's not here, does that make me patrol leader from now on?"

Scoutmaster Jeff scratched his chin while looking at me bewildered and said, "Uh…sure!"

It was obvious Scoutmaster Jeff had not noticed Jimmy's disappearance, nor had he given it much thought, either. Nonetheless, he had given me authority over my patrol. As I studied them I thought, "I'm now officially responsible for these guys. I have no idea what I'm doing, but I'm going to find out what I need to do and do it!"

When my mother came to pick me up after the meeting, I explained what happened, and that I needed to get a book on how to be a patrol leader right away. She agreed, and the next day we went to the scout store to find one.

The scout store had a book written specifically for patrol leaders. When I opened the book, I discovered it presented me with several ideas that would point me in the right direction. Two stood out immediately. First, the patrol leader had control over the decision regarding the mascot. Second, each patrol needed a flag.

I decided the squirrel had to go immediately, and I was grateful the rules allowed me to make that decision. Next, I had to do something about our flag. None of the other patrols had a flag, but that did not mean we couldn't carry one. In fact, I believed a flag would set us apart from the pack and give us our own unique identity.

I examined our options for a new patrol mascot. At the time, there were no dinosaur or dragon patches available, but had they been, one would have been my preferred choice. Reptiles fascinated me, but there was already a Cobra Patrol in our troop, so we could not have that one. We needed something that not only represented strength, but could also eat the other patrol mascots if they ever got into a competition.

Looking at all the various patches, something finally caught my eye. A patch with a green alligator baring its teeth definitely fit the bill. I bought ten gator patches, brought them to our next meeting, and handed them out to my patrol. "Guys, we're now the Gator Patrol of Troop 249," I said. The boys liked and approved of the idea, especially since it replaced the squirrel.

Then, as the new patrol leader, my next move was something that the world needs more of today. I took initiative. I went to Robby, our historian, and made him assistant patrol leader since he was second in line for seniority. Then, I said, "Guys, we need to get together this weekend at someone's house. It'll be just us. It won't be a troop function. But we need to get together to make a flag for our Gator Patrol."

Nick, the redhead, said, "We can do it at my house. My mom knows how to sew."

"Terrific!" I said. "I'll get the materials, and we'll figure it out when we get there."

After we arrived at Nick's house we worked up some designs for a flag, put together a pattern, and played video games while Nick's mom did the sewing. When she was done, we put it on a six-foot pole, and paraded around the outside of their house in perfect patrol fashion. The flag was a blue and red rectangle separated with a diagonal with a cutout of a mean, green gator on both sides.

As the patrol members each had a chance to hold their flag, I felt a feeling of pride forming among them. We were a part of something now, and the stories coming our way were entirely up to us. We weren't just any patrol in Troop 249. We were The Gator Patrol of

Troop 249! I eagerly awaited our next troop meeting, excited and curious to see how the rest of the troop would respond.

During our next meeting, we proudly hoisted our new flag into its stand. I kept my eyes on the other troop members, scanning their faces for their reactions. Two thought it was funny, but most simply stared in silence and admiration. Our scoutmasters congratulated us for taking the initiative and putting in the time and effort to make our flag. They were impressed with us. We surprised ourselves as well. We didn't do it because we were told to. We did it for ourselves.

When we sat down to begin the meeting, the flag still hung for the entire troop to see. It was almost as though it did our speaking for us. As the meeting progressed, I watched as members of the other patrols glanced at it, and then at us, from time to time. While we had a feeling of belonging, I wondered if some of the other boys wished they were in our patrol.

I also sensed some of the other patrol leaders did not like the fact that we took initiative. The leader of the Cobra Patrol, whose patrol had been around the longest and had the oldest boys, was particularly quiet. I got the impression the other patrols, were uncomfortable with or intimidated by our efforts as well, but I was not concerned. The members of the Gator Patrol were the people I was responsible for, and bringing them together was the right thing to do.

Leadership is a quality many people talk about, but most personally avoid. It is my opinion that our world is starving for good leadership. Leaders are often chosen by default simply because no one else is willing to stand up. Other times, there are people willing to stand up, but they have not educated themselves on how to lead. Most importantly, leaders must learn how to inspire and bring people together. The simple act of choosing our symbols created a message that began to build a culture among my patrol. One simple act such as that can begin to build a culture among other organizations, also.

As I saw our patrol come together, I became very proud of each of our members. I saw a bond forming amongst us as we learned to work together. However, the world is a fierce and wild place, full of many pitfalls and dangers. Little was I to know that our bond would be tested on my very first camping trip.

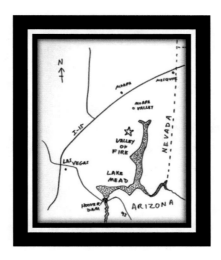

CHAPTER 4
VALLEY OF FIRE

AS THE MOON HUNG OVERHEAD on that cold desert night, thirty boys and their scoutmasters hiked along the lonely paved road. Each of us carried backpacks full of necessities. There were no lights except the quiet stars overhead. Occasionally, someone would pull out a flashlight to ascertain if a sound we heard was our imagination or was something real. More often than not, the sounds were imaginary as little moved during the winter night.

The trek through the Valley of Fire brought out the adventurer in me. The route to our campsite was short, only about three miles, but our leadership wanted us to experience the adventure of a night hike. They wanted us to learn to trust ourselves, trust our vision and our sense of direction, as well as Polaris, the North Star.

To this day, I can still find Polaris and determine my direction by first locating the most obvious constellation, Ursa Major, though it is more commonly referred to as the Big Dipper. Consisting of four bright stars positioned in the shape of a pan as viewed from the side, with an additional three bright stars protruding in a crooked line away from it, the Big Dipper is the easiest constellation to locate. When looked at together, the stars resemble the outline of a pan with a handle. When you look at the tip of the pan, you can draw a line from those two stars to another very bright star in the sky, Polaris, the North Star. Obviously, Polaris is important because when you can locate it, you can determine which way is north without the help of a compass. Then, you can ascertain which way is east, west, and south. As we hiked along this lonely road, Polaris was on my right, hanging in the sky above the dark shadows of the northern mountains. We continued to trek west towards a dirt road, which would lead us another mile towards our campsite.

At our campsite, we grouped into our patrols. The scoutmasters claimed their section, while each of the patrols found areas for themselves. We searched in the dark for space to pitch our tent. We needed space with little sagebrush, and often had to pull a bush or two from the ground to clear the space. Not all of the boys took the time to clear their space and spent the night sleeping on the lumpy sagebrush.

Pitching our tents in the dark was more difficult. The risk was that we might drop and lose a tent stake, never to be seen again as it lie buried underneath the desert sand. If the corners of the tent were not staked to the ground, the tent could come loose. If one of the boys rolled around, sleepless on the lumpy sagebrush, the tent could twist and contort. The noises of nature, the howl of a coyote, the hoot of an owl, or the scurrying of other animals through the brush could cause troop members to become restless and shift the tent out of its position. As we cleared our areas for the night, it was important for each boy to keep track of his tent stakes so that he would not awaken to a torn tent.

We built a fire and cooked our dinner in tin foil. After we ate, four of the older boys invited the rest of us to play a game of Capture the Flag. They created a team with just the four of them and wanted to play against the rest of the troop, a total of twenty-six boys. Surprisingly, four against twenty-six turned out to be a fair fight since they were faster and more athletic. Lacking the skill of navigating the terrain at night put us at a disadvantage. Cloaked in darkness, our only light was from the quarter moon, the stars, and the campfire.

We created a field boundary and decided that the edge of the mountains would be out of bounds. Large, black shadows of the mountains stood at a distance across the valley. We would not know until the next morning that we had just given ourselves a playing surface of several square miles.

The dirt road into the campsite defined "enemy territory". If a team member crossed into the enemy's territory and found himself captured, the enemy would put him in their jail. Since their jail was near the campfire, they would take us there and tempt us with S'mores, a delicious graham cracker, chocolate, and marshmallow delicacy. In our weakness, we would exchange hints to the whereabouts of our flag for a S'more or two. Then they would sneak to our side, steal our flag, and return it to their territory, shouting their triumphant victory.

They must have read Sun Tzu and the Art of War because they managed to win every game.

Before long, though, we all congregated by the campfire. Bob, Richie, Robby, Neil, Josh, and a new scout, Kory, and I would sit around the campfire and listen to the ghost stories our scoutmasters loved to tell. As the night wore on, one by one we retired to our tents, exhausted from excitement, yet somehow ready for the day ahead. All the while, the moon and the stars lit up the sky as the large mountainous shadows lurked in the distance.

The next day, having slept in our clothes from the night before, we threw on our hats over our unkempt hair and cooked our breakfast over the campfire. The winter chill tugged at our bones, and it surprised me how cold it could get in the desert. It was early, and not an animal or bird stirred. It was a land at sleep, and somehow we were in the middle of it. The sun came from the west, from the other side of the rock wall next to our campsite, only it was not just a wall. It was a massive mountain, and the shade it produced intensified the chilly air.

As daylight spread throughout the valley, the mountains appeared to be much farther away than they had at night. The sagebrush, brown from its cool winter hibernation, spread liberally across the valley floor. Sandstone plateaus, rock protrusions that jetted from the middle of the desert sand, flooded the central valley and stood forty to sixty feet high, with jagged cliff walls protruding from their edges. I felt like I stood in some long lost era, a witness to the remnant left after the Paleozoic sea receded into what is now the Pacific Ocean. If we had looked closely at their outer walls, I am sure we would have discovered fossils of some long lost creatures. However, being the boys that we were, all we wanted to do was to climb on top of the valley rocks and examine the view from up high.

That morning, the scoutmasters had planned a lesson on how to use our compasses. The lesson required us to hike back to the paved road and run through a pre-planned compass obstacle course. We finished just before lunch, and after we cooked our noon meal, we explored the valley. All of us gravitated to the nearest sandstone plateau, approximately one half mile from our campsite. Three sides of that particular plateau ended in a steep cliff with overhanging edges. From below, I imagined myself standing on the plateau and peeking over the highest edge. I figured I'd find myself looking down a fifty-foot drop, with nothing but hard rock, sand, and sagebrush below. A fall would definitely cause serious injury, or even death, if any of us lost our balance and fell over the edge.

On the northern edge, however, was a crevasse that, if managed correctly, would allow us to climb to the top. We figured out the crevasse and one by one we managed to reach the heights of the plateau. The view from the top stretched for miles. Majestic mountains enclosed the valley below us. As I looked across the horizon, I gained a new awareness of nature and felt closer to God up there. As large as the mountains were, they had been placed there to serve us rather than for us to serve them.

Our campsite was to the east, and the rock wall next to our campfire was less intimidating. It appeared more like a protector against the raw, wintry wind. Up there, our perspectives changed. We were no longer lost in the night. Instead, we saw what was real, and the land that day was for us and us alone.

A loud whistle at the campsite called our attention. One of the assistant scoutmasters had learned the art of whistling loudly to get attention and alert us to return to camp. We took our turns descending the crevasse, and made our way back to our scoutmasters. After most of the boys hurried across the valley floor back to camp, Richie, Robby, Kory, and I still had not yet made the descent. Richie climbed down, and then Robby. I looked at Kory, and he said he wanted to look at the view one more time, so I worked my way down the plateau. I found the ground, walked a circle around the plateau, and turned to head back to camp. Suddenly, from around the corner, I heard some loose pebbles and a nervous, "Whooooaaaaaa," from the plateau up above.

I paused to listen while my hairs stiffened behind my neck. Though the noises stopped, I returned to the plateau to investigate. I called Kory's name, but there was no answer. Something was wrong. I went around to the west side of the plateau and called Kory's name again. This time, Kory responded, "Yes," up above, his voice barely louder than a whisper. I glanced upward, against the bright blue sky, and I saw two legs and shoes hanging over the edge of the plateau. Kory, too close to the edge, had slipped, leaving his body dangling fifty feet above with his fingers clawing into the sandstone. He yelled for help, afraid that he would plummet into the impenetrable valley floor below.

"Hang on, Kory!" I yelled. Then I pivoted back toward the camp and shouted, "Robby, Richie, get back here! Kory needs help, right now!" I rushed back to the crevasse and raced back up to the top of the plateau. When I found him, Kory was in a far worse place than I imagined, his body pressed tightly against a flat edge of the rock that angled downward. The rocks surrounding him were loose, and I guessed that they were the reason he had slipped. Fortunately, he'd found a small weed growing from the rock that he held onto with all his might. It was just enough to stop sliding. His torso flattened against the loose edge, and his legs flailed over the empty air below. Kory's life hung from that rock and could have ended in seconds.

My mind raced, searching for ways to help my fellow scout. Robby had reached the top of the plateau, but he was small, only about half my size. Because of the condition of the rocks, we knew Kory's rescuer could easily fall along with our friend, but I was sure, if we worked together, we could save him. We formed a small human chain of sorts as Richie made his way up the crevasse. When he saw Kory hanging over the edge, he reacted. Not worried about loose rocks, sloping angles, or cliffs, he stepped onto the flat, reached down, grabbed Kory by the collar, and pulled him to safety. I watched with trepidation, worried he might fall and take Kory with him, but Richie didn't fall. Nor did he act afraid. He simply reacted, just as his mother had when her son ran onto the soccer field. Richie had just saved Kory's life.

Kory, shaking and nervous, was thankful he had not fallen the fifty feet to his possible demise. Quick, high-pitched laughter gave away our nervousness, but we kept our tone light, ribbing Kory for doing too much sightseeing. The walk back to the campsite was quiet, each knowing something special had just transpired between us, something that changed us permanently. I commended Richie for his actions again, but he just shrugged it off and said he was glad everyone was alright. We never mentioned Kory's near death experience to our scoutmasters, but that night, as we played another round of Capture the Flag, I understood how different things could have been.

That experience taught me how quickly the world can come down upon us. How, in an instant we could be at the top of the plateau overlooking the horizon, and a second later, that same plateau could threaten our very existence. Only with the help of others can we survive those moments when the world shows its vengeance. Those of us in a position of aid can help in one of two ways. Like Robby and myself, through thoughtful action, or as Richie did, through immediate action. Though I am not sure which is the better choice, I believe they are both options coming from a good place.

When the problem occurred, we took different approaches to solve it. Robby and I hoped we had time to get to Kory, and keep everyone safe in the process. Richie, on the other hand, felt there was no time, and risked further injury to achieve the same result. Regardless of our technique, we all worked toward the same objective. Thankfully, each of us made it back to camp in one piece.

As I look to leadership positions today, I often reflect on that episode. As much as I thought my way was the right way, Richie showed me that his way worked just as well. When I work with other people today, I make sure I'm open to their point of view and the solutions that they have in mind. I may think of a way to achieve the objective, but someone else may have a way to achieve the same result more effectively. If the end result is satisfactory, that's fine with me. Just get it done successfully.

As we hopped in the cars the following Sunday and began our trip back home, I thought about all the different ways to achieve an objective. The Valley of Fire showed us just how quickly things could change. I admired Richie for his action, even though I didn't know what we would have done if he had slipped and fallen. On that drive home, I realized that future adventures would be in store for our troop, and we would have input as to what those were. Being a patrol leader, I knew I'd have some ideas. Still, I thought how I wanted to be sure everyone had a part in what we would put on our calendar. After all, someone might have an idea that I had not considered.

CHAPTER 5
PLANNING

THE AIR STILL HAD A CHILL   on that Saturday morning. When I arrived at the house, I noticed that it was modest. The inside was about what you'd expect from any dual working family with teenage kids.   There was not much in the way of aesthetics, except for pictures hung on the wall, awards from some past accomplishments, and some plants scattered in various places. Most of the house was designed for comfort and efficiency. Despite this, there were papers scattered around.   I could tell that the hectic schedules of all the home's residents kept efficiency at bay.   Most of the papers sat on the top of the kitchen table, but the dining room table on this day was not much better.

It was my first troop leadership meeting. The meeting was called to plan our troop activities for the next year, six months, and three months, with our scoutmaster there to guide us. Long term goals might only get a calendar date, but they were given a date, nonetheless. Short term goals were also given calendar dates, but more attention was given to their planning. We needed to outline specific activities on a checklist, and determine the appropriate person responsible for those activities.

One by one, the troop leaders walked into the house. Bob and Richie already sat in their seats. Josh arrived soon after, as did Neil. Robby, my assistant, took his seat next to me. Eventually, Scoutmaster Jeff cleared the papers off the dining room table, and threw other papers on top of it. At his command, we each took a seat around the table. Though our Scoutmaster Jeff was there, he knew it was only his job to oversee the meeting. The actual planning was left to us boys. As I looked around the table, I saw a strong group. Together we would make a plan of action for the coming months. Our discussion that day determined whether we, as a group, went forward or backward. It all depended on us.

I did not know what to expect from my first meeting. It was possible the leadership council had already assumed a course of action. I expected not much would change since, so far, I had thought the camping trips and experiences we'd had were exceptional. Choosing a good troop was vital because if they were already doing the right things, the best course of action would be to stay on that path. I decided that, as they ran through our troop activities, I would volunteer my patrol to complete some of the action items that needed to be completed. I did not plan to volunteer for them all, but I knew that if I volunteered first, I could decide what we would do. Those that did not speak up would have to take the items nobody wanted.

However, I had an idea I wanted to present. It was an idea I felt would not affect the troop, per se, but would contribute to my patrol's growth.

"Alright," said Bobby. "As acting senior patrol leader, I guess we'd better get going."

A silence permeated the room. I looked from scout to scout, and was unsure of what should come next. Being my first meeting, I sat quietly as I felt it would be better to observe.

Finally, Bobby said, "How do we start?"

Then Scoutmaster Jeff spoke up, "If I may make a suggestion. This is a boy's planning process, but I'm here to help guide you. Usually, when we begin planning, we look at three things. First, what recommended activities do we have from the national organization. Then, we look at what is recommended or available from the local organization. And, finally, we look at the goals we have set for ourselves."

"Makes sense," Richie said.

"What types of things do we have coming from national?" Josh asked. He looked at Bob, who shrugged and averted his eyes to our scoutmaster.

"What about Philmont?" Neil asked.

Philmont Scout Ranch, located in the Sangre de Cristo Mountains of the Rocky Mountains in northern New Mexico, was a high adventure camp owned by the Boy Scouts of America. Twelve miles wide and thirty miles long, the range was home to six rugged peaks made for high adventure hiking. Its highest peak, Mount Baldy, stood at 12,441 feet. Mount Charleston, the highest peak just west of our homes in Las Vegas, stood at 11,916 feet, so we felt that climbing Mount Baldy at Philmont Scout Ranch would be quite an accomplishment.

"Nah, I don't think we're ready for that one just yet," Richie said.

He was probably right. We had several young, new members of the troop, and preparing for a trek like Philmont's Mount Baldy required many practice hikes. Instead, we examined the upcoming popcorn fundraiser, and the best popcorn sales locations to raise money for future camping trips.

We also had to plan and schedule food drives that required us to leave bags on people's front door handles, then return two weeks later to collect the filled bags from those who wished to donate.

There were two local events planned. The local scout organization had scheduled our Jamboree, a night of camping on the field of the Las Vegas Stars minor league baseball team, now known as the Area 51s. We placed the Jamboree on the calendar and assigned troop members with responsibilities.

Caesar's Palace officials asked us to install thousands of miniature American flags around their fountains for the July Fourth celebration. After we completed that task, they would treat us to a buffet meal and a show inside the OmniMax, a spherical theatre that displayed the highest resolution educational programming available at the time.

"So, what are *our* goals?" I asked, assuming we would address them next.

Richie replied, "Our primary goal is Eagle advancement. We want all the members of our troop to advance to the rank of Eagle Scout. One of the best ways we can do that is by sending us all to summer camp. That's why we have our popcorn sales. Other than that, we want to be a high adventure troop, meaning we try to go on a camping trip at least one night per month. Sometimes it'll be two nights, but we'll go for at least one."

"With that being said," Bob interrupted, "where do we want to go camping?"

We discussed potential locations and tentatively scheduled those we liked best for later in the year. We planned our summer camp locations, as well as their alternatives. We determined who would be responsible for food, transportation, equipment, and merit badges for the next six months of activities.

I understood what the future held, but I wanted more for my own patrol. I looked at Scoutmaster Jeff and asked, "Sir, I want to know if my patrol can have our own camping trips."

"Show off," said Josh under his breath. He snickered and rolled his eyes.

"Well, I think that would be a great idea," Jeff said. "In fact, there is one more activity our troop has been asked to perform. We have been asked to oversee a garage sale at a house on the other side of the airport and, seeing as how well your patrol is being run, I think your patrol can take the first shift. That involves setting up everything the evening before, and camping out front to keep watch. Are you up for it?"

"Sounds good to me!" I said.

The other boys rolled their eyes, but I thought it would be perfect. Our patrol would have our own campout. It would be just us and our green gator flag. It would strengthen our bonds, and make us a better team.

"We're up for it, Sir. Put us down on the calendar!"

During that meeting I learned how planning starts with generalities first, and then progresses to a more narrowed approach, focusing on each separate event, with tasks assigned along the way. I was excited about where our troop's direction, and how my patrol would be a strong faction within it.

As it would so happen, we did begin to find our strength at the garage sale event, but not in the way I had anticipated. Unfortunately even the best laid plans can all fall apart due to the selfish actions of a single individual. In fact, our troop's very existence would be put to the test, and not everyone would remain afterwards.

CHAPTER 6
CORRUPTION

ON CLEAR NIGHTS when the Las Vegas sky faded from blue to bright orange to red to black, only the strongest stars were able to permeate the downtown lights of the casinos. Each night, the casino lights served as a glowing dome above the city, a defense against the natural light above. The artificial lights attracted tourists across the globe for gambling, adventure, and fun.

Tourism had always been the primary industry in the state of Nevada, with Las Vegas being one of the world's tourist meccas. Restaurant owners, car dealers, homebuilders, carpenters, educators, painters, and people of other countless professions came to the Las Vegas valley to support the tourist industry and gain a part of its wealth.

Much like the gold rush brought people from the east into California, the Valley became home to many first generation families, and understandably so. Once California was settled, people moved to Las Vegas in droves in the hopes of achieving fortune. Billboards and monstrous neon signs have drawn people to the city with the promise of making millions with the drop of a few coins into a slot machine. The idea of fortune was everywhere. As more and more homes sprouted up across the desert, Clark County became the fastest growing county in the United States.

The allure of wealth and good fortune associated with living in Las Vegas mattered more than heritage, as the city was a true melting pot. Skin color was irrelevant. In fact, some people dressed in so much purple you couldn't tell what skin color they had. The only colors that mattered were the green in your wallet, the silver of your coins, or the color of your credit cards. Culture wasn't what brought you to the city. Either you came to Las Vegas with your family for the chance at a better life, or you left your family to come for the promise of an opportunity.

Unfortunately, the allure of wealth exposed the shortcomings of human nature. With it came vices, which created a suggestive subculture of questionable behavior. Not all gamblers became addicts, but those who succumbed to the addiction of the roll of the dice could end up destroying their soul as well as the lives of the ones they love.

As I matured, I realized there were two types of gamblers living in Las Vegas, those who were professionals or those with an addiction. Billboards for casinos offering the chance to win millions stood alongside billboards providing solutions for addiction recovery.

And then there was the skin. Billboards of scantily clad women crowded the sky along the main thoroughfare of the city known as Las Vegas Boulevard, but more frequently referred to as "The Strip". The nickname wasn't an accident. A quick drive along The Strip led to sights of suggestive pictures of women on taxi cabs, on the signs of the casinos, or, even worse, on fliers stapled to poles along the sidewalks of the street. Those fliers were the most suggestive.

Fortunately, the magnitude of this subculture created a counter culture of people who made a different choice. A city's reputation did not determine the quality of each city resident. In fact, I knew many strong individuals who stood for their faith more forcefully simply because their morality was tested so blatantly.

Various churches of all denominations were filled with members who actively helped those in need. Though the allure of Las Vegas promised wealth, power, and perfection, many of its residents knew a softer reality.

Growing up in Las Vegas, one could find temptation around every corner. My friends and I had witnessed both the destruction of temptation, but also the saving power of humanity. Unlike the judgment handed down from outsiders, as residents we identified ourselves in the community by our actions. We owned our reputations in Las Vegas. Either we chose to be moral, or we did not. Either we would build each other up, or we'd perform acts that would hurt one another. Each night, under the glowing dome of the casino lights, this battle of principles waged fiercely. It was under this glowing dome that my Gator Patrol camped on the front yard grass getting ready for the next day's garage sale.

The troop had been growing under the leadership of our scoutmasters. By the time this night came upon us, my patrol was about ten members strong. Other patrols grew their membership as well. Three brothers, Russ, Kevin, and Jesse, joined the troop when their father moved to Las Vegas as an Airman for Nellis Air Force Base. The scoutmasters separated the three into different patrols and their father, Dan, quickly became an assistant scoutmaster. Since our troop's reputation became one of high standards, others begrudgingly came to Troop 249 because their parents felt they needed a more positive influence. One boy in particular was teetering on the edge of attending boarding school.

While we set up the garage sale tables, Kevin asked, "Do the lights ever go away here?"

"No," I said. "They're always on every night."

"You can't even see the stars that well," Russ said.

"Sort of makes it hard to get that Astronomy merit badge," said Robby. We all had a laugh and after making sure our tent stakes were firmly in the ground, we turned in for the night.

The following morning, the sun rose over Lake Mead, and the sky was cloudless as usual. Fortunately, we did not get much rain in Las Vegas, and that made choosing camping dates easy. We felt we never really had to worry about the weather, though we knew we had to prepare for flash floods if ever there was a threat of rain. Since it only rained a few times per year, odds were that we would have a dry campsite whenever we chose to go.

As the sun climbed above the eastern mountains, we set up the garage sale. Tables and chairs, price tags, and all sorts of equipment conformed into a flowing outdoor retail outlet. Jesse and Kevin put up the tables. Robby helped learn how to run the cash register, and Russ and I marked prices on the tags and put them on the appropriate items. The owner of the house went to a local fast food joint and brought us breakfast. As the chill of the morning quickly wore off, our Gator Patrol flag hung in the sky above a group of scouts ready for the work ahead.

The plan was simple. Our patrol had the first shift. We would run the garage sale until about eleven. At that time, the Cobra Patrol would come and relieve us, and the Gator Patrol members would be free to go. Shortly after we set up the sale, people began to find their way to us. The house was not hard to find. There were few trees around the roadways, so a simple cardboard sign sufficed, announcing that our garage sale appeared straight ahead. It was not long until customers came and we got into a rhythm of selling goods and collecting cash.

Time can fly when you get into that rhythm, but eventually one of the assistant scoutmasters suggested each of us take quick, individual breaks and head inside and get some water. I suggested I go last, as I wanted my patrol to go ahead of me. When it was my turn to go, I went into the house and walked by the kitchen. There on the kitchen table sat an open purse, which I assumed must be that of Scoutmaster Jeff's wife, who had just arrived to help. There was no one else around, and I thought to myself that maybe she'd be coming back soon. I thought it didn't seem to be the smartest thing to do to leave her purse sitting out where it was. Shaking my head, I passed the table and walked into the kitchen where I grabbed a glass of water, guzzled it down, and returned to my garage sale duties.

The scoutmaster's wife stood near the driveway, talking with the house owner. Not wanting to interrupt, I edged near them as they continued their conversation. Right then a couple of cars pulled up. It was the Cobra Patrol and an assistant scoutmaster. The homeowner told the kids to put their things inside, and then come back out so they could take over the duties. I looked at the members of the Cobra Patrol. They were bigger kids, and slightly older than the rest of us. One of them in particular was new, and I felt he fit into the category of becoming a scout rather than going to boarding school. Since it was getting chaotic, I felt I needed to help restore some order and I went back to my responsibilities. During the transition, kids ran in and out of the house and learned how to run the garage sale. Inside sat an unguarded purse.

Once the transition was completed, the Gator Patrol went our separate ways. After saying our goodbyes, my mother drove me home. However, a few minutes after getting home, the phone rang. It was the scoutmaster's wife. She told my mother that $300 disappeared from her purse, and I needed to come back right then. I felt a twinge of apprehension, because I knew she suspected everyone, including me, though I had taken nothing. I immediately had my suspicions as to who would have taken it, but there was no way to prove it. Could it have been the boarding school candidate? I felt confident no one from my patrol would have done it, but there was no way to know for sure.

Back at the garage sale, the scoutmaster's wife was frantic. The mood was completely different. Not only had she called back each member of the Gator Patrol, but she'd called the police too, and they were there, preparing to question each of us individually. My patrol and I looked at each other with shifting eyes. Who was it? Was it more than one? Was she making the whole thing up? Why was this happening? What will happen next?

"I bet it's the new kid," whispered one kid. "I don't trust that kid."

"How do we know it's not you?" whispered another.

"Be quiet!"

"Well, how do we know *he* isn't the one who took it?"

"Guys, this won't solve anything," I said. "If you have it, just turn it in and nothing will happen."

"Are you kidding?" another member said. "Whoever took it isn't going to turn it in, not with all these adults and the police here."

"Yea, it would be too hard for whoever took it to fess up under all these conditions."

They questioned all of us and searched our pockets, but the money never turned up. The police told us that we could all go home. Later that night, we received another phone call. Due to the events of the morning, Scoutmaster Jeff had decided to resign his post as scoutmaster, and he would leave Troop 249 immediately. The troop council would determine a new leader shortly, but we were to come to the next meeting as planned.

When I retired to bed that evening, I felt sad. Our troop had done great things. My patrol had grown and gained a positive reputation. Suddenly, with the betrayal of our scoutmaster and the troop in peril,

I felt troubled as leader of my patrol. Since my patrol had been at the house the longest, I could not help but think if one of my friends was to blame. I suspected the boarding school candidate, but without proof, I could not be sure.

The incident had a chaotic effect on our troop. We struggled to find a new scoutmaster, until Richie's father, Chuck, volunteered. The troop's confidence was shattered. Many of us questioned the importance of the group and wondered how something like that could happen in the scouts. We also worried whether one act of corruption could topple the whole system. Meeting attendance dropped, and several of the boys, including our senior patrol leader, left Troop 249 completely.

We never saw the boarding school candidate again.

Pondering these events a few weeks later, I came to realize that no organization is invulnerable to corruption. Evil exists in the absence of good, but good doesn't just exist in the absence of evil. The leaders are responsible for creating the culture of good, and, though it takes much effort, they must constantly point to virtue in order to protect their organizations. Then, their people must willfully choose virtue over temptation. Unfortunately, for my troop, one member did the opposite.

I wondered what, then, is the best way to overcome that corruption. Had we not done a good thing, and raised money through a garage sale? Due to one selfish act, our troop had changed. How, then, could we protect ourselves? As my thoughts about life turned to these questions, I drifted off to sleep. Outside my window, the glow of the Las Vegas lights fought its nightly battle against the stars above

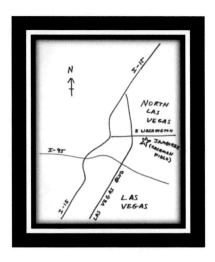

CHAPTER 7
LIFE

CHUCK'S ACCEPTANCE of the scoutmaster role returned some stability to our troop. A painter by trade, Chuck also volunteered for his Catholic church, pondering often its teachings within the challenges of life. Still, Chuck dedicated himself to service, and both he and his wife and family became heavily involved in our troop. A good man, it gladdened me that he chose to guide us.

After Bob had left, Chuck informed the assistant senior patrol leader that he would assume command as the new senior patrol leader. Unfortunately, the young man's eyes widened and a look of dread fell over his face. He resigned from his post and the troop a few weeks later, and Troop 249 remained without a senior patrol leader until the next election.

In the meantime, however, we had our plan. Our direction from national and regional had not changed, and we still had our goals to get us all to Eagle and to be a high adventure troop. With so much turmoil, staying focused on the plan was critical. Surviving the chaos required that we rebuild the bonds between us. Scoutmaster Chuck called a meeting for all the patrol leaders, and we each made a commitment to each other.

The next big item scheduled on the calendar was the local Jamboree. The Jamboree, an annual event held in the outfield of the Las Vegas Stars minor league baseball field, brought together all the troops in the city to share ideas, show off talents, play games, and enjoy the outdoors. A convention of sorts, we always left with new friends and new scout skills.

Some troops demonstrated their knot tying abilities, making bridges, teepees, and large forts out of ropes and heavy logs. Others exhibited charts of local animals, star constellations, geology, and maps. Our troop displayed our compass skills, creating an obstacle course, which sent scouts through the chaos to various troop campsites and then back to us, checking off their experiences along the way. If they successfully completed the course, we would give a small token of achievement such as a patch or a certificate.

Sean, one of our newer scouts, loved the adventure of exploring. More so, however, he loved exploring quickly. He had it in his mind that no matter the obstacle course, he would complete it faster than anybody else would. Breathing quickly from running through the course, Sean returned with his compass checklist in his hand and a big smile on his face.

"That was a piece of cake!" Sean said.

"Sean, you're supposed to enjoy the experience and learn something from the other troops," said Scoutmaster Chuck.

"Oh, I did learn something," he replied. "I just learned it faster than everybody else!"

"Alright. Then why don't you go explore again, and bring us back something?"

"Where should I go?" We learned early on that Sean was dependable only so long as you gave him clear and specific instructions. If our directions were vague, there was no telling how he would surprise us.

"I've been looking for one of those glow sticks that I've seen some of the other kids with," I said. "Can you find out who has them and how we can get them?"

"I'm on it!" Sean said, and he turned and ran back into the chaos.

After Sean disappeared from view behind the giant teepee, Chuck said, "Good thinking. Now we need to think of something else for him as soon as he gets back."

As the sun disappeared over the mountains, the scouts gathered around a fire pit for dinner. We said grace in the form of "Yay God! Let's eat!" and after dinner we eventually settled in for the night. The echoes of excitement bounced off the outfield walls, though slowly they vanished into silence.

The next morning we said a prayer and ceremoniously raised the American flag. Rows of scouts saluted the flag upon its rise, and finished with the Pledge of Allegiance. I appreciated the ceremony prior to the day, as I wondered how many other young men in the world could not participate in similar events because they lacked freedom within their own country. After breakfast, our events commenced. We competed in three-legged races, potato sack races, knot tying races, compass races, and bridge crossing races. With all the competition involving speed, Sean felt like he had died and gone to heaven. He thrived and excelled at each race he entered.

Under the cover of our tent, we sat on lawn chairs with Scoutmaster Chuck. He began a deep conversation with us about religion and philosophy, discussing the human experience and our relationships to God and each other. Most of us had more questions than answers. Looking back, I realize it was in the seeking of those answers that my faith grew.

As the sun set beyond the western mountains, I could sense the energy dissipate among the campers.

"It's almost time to break camp," Scoutmaster Chuck said.

"If it's alright with you, I'd like to take one last walk around before we do," I said.

"Go right ahead, but try to be back in thirty minutes."

"Will do," I said, and I turned around and began to walk.

While I strolled through the campsites, I wanted to observe the actions of the other troops. Though their display booths were impressive, I was more interested in whether or not the scouts themselves were cohesive. I asked many questions during my walk. What was their culture? Did they get along? Did they respect their leaders? Why did they choose their patrol names? Were the boys advancing in rank towards Eagle? I realized that tired troops had a hard time hiding their true character. All the boys worked in unison in one troop, while another troop's leaders tried to break up a fight. Some campsites were clean and orderly. Other campsites had no organization at all.

In the middle of all the chaos, a tall scoutmaster wearing a cowboy hat walked towards me. He was clean-shaven, and his shadow stretched long against the western sun. He wore his scoutmaster uniform proudly, and something about it caused me to pause. Scouts wore their rank patches on their left pockets where scoutmasters did not typically wear patches. However, this one wore a rank patch on his left pocket for all to see.

The rank patches were Scout, Tenderfoot, Second Class, First Class, Star, Life, and then Eagle. The earlier ranks were more common, but after Star, the Life and Eagle patches were few and far between. Life patches were bright red in the shape of a heart. When I saw one of those, I knew that Eagle was close at hand for that young man. The Eagle patches were very rare. Usually when a boy made Eagle, they were older and would move onto other things. An Eagle patch was a significant achievement, a goal reached by few. When I saw one, I was inspired.

As the scoutmaster and I crossed paths, the red heart of the Life patch continued to grab my attention. I thought it strange that this rugged looking Scoutmaster would wear a patch made for boys. He had to have a story to tell.

"Excuse me, Sir," I said. "I noticed that you're wearing the Life patch on your shirt. I just thought that was unusual. Do you mind my asking you why?"

"Well," he said humbly, "when I was a scout, I made it all the way to Life, but then I quit. I never achieved my rank of Eagle, and I've always regretted it every day since."

As I stood there looking at him, I could see the hurt in his eyes. He continued, "The only way I could alleviate some of my pain was to help others to not make the same mistake that I did. I wear this patch to remind you boys to keep going until you achieve the rank of Eagle. I can't go back and change it for me, but I can help others, so that's why I wear it."

I paused, not quite knowing what to say. Finally, I said, "That's a great message for your boys. They are lucky to have a guy like you to help lead them."

"Thank you."

The sadness in his eyes for not achieving Eagle was obvious. So also was his hope of redemption. I would never forget those emotions after we parted ways.

If there ever was an Honorary Eagle award, this man should have had it, but it does not work that way. In order for an achievement to have meaning, a scout must earn it, not have it handed to him.

An achievement takes work and sacrifice, drive and determination. We get one shot in life to achieve something special. While we work toward the achievement, life will throw us obstacles to make us doubt the worth of its completion. Those doubts seem to hit us hardest right before we finish the task. Maybe we mature through the process and start dreaming of other things. Maybe we begin to feel that the patch is just a patch, and there is really no meaning behind it.

More prominently, I believe the world wants us to avoid the chance to become exceptional. If we become exceptional, we are not like all the rest. We will stand out from the crowd, and we will be accountable. It is scary to stand apart, and sometimes those deep seeded fears enter our mindset in the form of "It's not worth it," or "It's just a patch," or "I've got other things I'd like to do."

Then we have missed our chance. Our work to become exceptional has ended before we reached our goal. We feel justified because we stayed with the crowd. However, the future can be cruel. Over time, we look back and realize we lost an opportunity. We no longer want to be like everybody else, but by then it's too late. The achievement that would have set us apart is off in the distant past, along with the future opportunities that would have come only with its completion.

I believe the Boy Scouts gave the Life patch its name for a reason. We determine our lives by whether or not we choose to be our best. Reaching Life is the most critical time for a Boy Scout. We will have to choose. Will we finish the goal, or will we not? No one else can make the choice for us.

In a very courageous and humble display, the Scoutmaster I met showed me that choice, and the consequences of choosing not to achieve Eagle. His regret may never have left him, but his decision to wear the Life patch inspired others to complete their goal. When life forced its choice on me, his display helped me to push through just as I am sure it did the members of his own troop.

However, his message inspired another thought within me. I realized the same message needed to spread to the members of my troop, and I knew I was capable of making it happen. By that point, I had yet to see anyone from our troop become an Eagle, or even come close to it. That had to change. I decided to leave my Gator Patrol and run for the position of senior patrol leader. I felt it was time for me to be the leader of Troop 249. In doing so, however, I would quickly realize I still had much to learn.

The Scout Motto

Be
Prepared!

CHAPTER 8
THE VOTE

EVERY SIX MONTHS, Troop 249 held elections. On election night after the initial proceedings, each candidate spoke to the troop. When it was time to vote, the boys wrote their choice on a piece of paper and handed it back to the scoutmasters to tally. While the scoutmasters counted the votes, the scouts stayed outside and played a game. Not much time would pass before the scoutmasters called back the boys to take their seats inside the trailer. The scoutmaster announced the new winner, and after a brief applause, the winner announced his assistant. Afterwards, proceedings for patrol leaders took place, and new leaders announced. Once the meeting ended, the new leaders gathered to discuss a new direction.

Among the patrol leaders, I felt I had the most momentum. My Gator Patrol had grown quickly and our flag had garnished a reputation, even getting recognition among other troops in the Las Vegas valley. At one point during the Jamboree, for example, I overheard some scouts from an entirely different troop talk about our Gator Patrol, how they were impressed with what we were doing, and that they decided to make their own flag. Having overcome the garage sale incident, I felt we had built a positive reputation within the entire city, let alone Troop 249.

The decision to run for a leadership position is not an easy one. It often starts with a feeling, something compelling, a driving force that soon develops into the reason. With the newfound purpose come ideas and plans that the potential leader must effectively sell as a vision to his constituents. What is ironic is that the plans and ideas create the vision, yet the vision is not about ideas or plans. A vision is a feeling given to others. The plans and ideas may change, as circumstances change, but the feeling needs to stay the same for those who elected you. The promise is not so much in the plans but in the feeling, the vision created.

As patrol leader, I felt our Gator Patrol set a higher standard. With the garage sale incident well behind us, I could see our patrol was outperforming all the rest. We scheduled our own campouts. We accepted the most challenging volunteer activities. Our boys advanced in rank at a rapid pace. Most importantly, we stuck together and created a bond between us.

On a couple of occasions, a scout from another patrol confided in me that he wanted to come over to our patrol. Sadly, I felt I could not do that to a fellow patrol leader, as I believed the switch would have caused discord among the troop. I decided that in order to give our scouts the best experience possible, I would have to lead the troop. When Scoutmaster Chuck called for senior patrol leader nominations, I raised my hand to nominate myself as a senior patrol leader candidate. Surprisingly, my long-time friend Richie raised his hand to nominate himself as well.

Richie and I had been friends for years. We were both big kids and we both expressed similar philosophical views. He was the patrol leader of his patrol, and they were a good group. However, I did not feel they were the same caliber as mine.

Unlike me, however, Richie was a lifer. He had begun his scouting career the first day he was eligible to join the Cub Scouts. After advancing through the Cub Scouts, he moved rapidly through the ranks as a Boy Scout. His longevity as a scout afforded him a higher rank on his shirt and approximately one-third more merit badges on his green sash than me. Richie had saved Kory's life and with a father as scoutmaster and a family devoted to the troop, he was a solid opponent.

I held a great deal of respect for Richie. "If I'm not going to win," I thought, "then Richie will definitely deserve it."

However, a second later another thought occurred to me. "When *I* win, though, Richie will make a great assistant senior patrol leader."

"And now," Scoutmaster Chuck said, "Our two candidates will give their speeches. We'll let Richie go first"

Richie stood up, his covered sash displaying all his merit badges. "I'm glad to be running for senior patrol leader," he said. "I've been doing this a long time, and I've seen a lot. I have more merit badges than anyone in the troop, and I've been a patrol leader for a long time. I have the experience to help all of you get your merit badges and to rank advance more quickly so that we will all get to Eagle. I feel I'm the most experienced to help you reach your goals."

After he spoke, Richie sat down and it was my turn.

"I admit that I don't have the experience that Richie has," I began, "but if you look at the Gator Patrol, you can see the things that we're doing. Our members are advancing quickly, and our patrol is doing all kinds of things not only within the troop but also outside of it. I want to take our troop to the next level. I want us to be known not only as the best troop in Las Vegas, but also in the entire southwest. I believe we can do it, and I'm ready for the challenge."

When I was done, I sat down. The speech, I thought, was good. Richie's uniform did most of his talking, though. It was momentum versus experience. From the looks on the faces of Troop 249, I felt I had the election won. Richie would be my assistant, and we would be on our way.

However, for some reason I began to wonder if Richie would be hurt if he lost. I wanted his buy-in. He was a strong person, and if he believed we should do something differently than I, there could be conflict. Therefore, I thought it over, and I made a plan. I was certain I had the votes to win, so I decided to vote for Richie out of respect. That way, I could honestly tell him I voted for him because of his experience, and he would be more amenable to working with me.

"Alright then," Scoutmaster Chuck said. "We're going to pass out the ballots. Each of you will write down the name you choose for senior patrol leader, fold your papers, and pass them to the front."

"I'm voting for Superman!" said Kevin. I heard giggles throughout the room.

"You can vote for Superman if you want, but know that what you do determines the direction of your troop for the next six months."

As the boys received their ballots, the room quieted down. One by one they wrote with their pencils, folded their ballots, and passed them to the front. The scoutmasters collected all the ballots, and they dismissed us for our outside break. Inside the trailer, the scoutmasters counted the votes, while outside the scouts played a game of Capture the Flag.

Everyone but Richie and I played the game. We were both nervous, and neither of us felt much like running around. At one point, Sean sprinted up to me and said, "I voted for you."

"I would hope so," I replied. "You're in my patrol!"

Sean smiled, turned, and ran again. He always seemed to want to run, and I smiled at how each of our members had different talents, which made us strong when brought together.

A few minutes later, we assembled inside our trailer. Each of the boys took their seats among their patrols, while Richie and I stood along the wall, waiting for the outcome.

Scoutmaster Chuck walked in, followed by his assistants. "Men, it was a very close race," he began. "But, the winner…by one vote…is Richie!"

Amidst the cheers and congratulations, I stood before them, shocked.

One vote? *My vote*!

My vote for Richie cost me the chance at making the difference I wanted to make. I looked at Richie, congratulated him, and just shook my head. How could I have overthought it like that? Look what I lost by making my vote. Unbelievable!

"Now Richie, it's time for you to select your assistant," said a scoutmaster.

"Well, I've thought this over, and with all the things he's been able to do in such a short amount of time, I select Matt to be my assistant senior patrol leader." He turned to me and said, "Matt, will you accept the position to be my assistant?"

"I will," I said.

"Men," said Chuck, "you now have before you your new leadership of Troop 249. Congratulate them, and let's separate into our patrols to pick your new patrol leaders."

The boys issued a "Congratulations!", yet inside I was numb. I had lost because I gave it to him. Assured of the votes going my way, I discounted his experience far too much. One vote, just one, gave Richie his chance to lead the troop, and my chance would have to take a backseat for another six months. What's more, I let down all those who voted for me and placed their hopes in me. I could blame no one but myself. I felt awful.

I learned from this a valuable lesson, one that still haunts me today. All votes are final, and every one of them counts. If you are running for a position, voting for a candidate, or voting on an issue, your vote will remain in force until the next time to vote comes around, if it ever does. All elections have consequences.

In addition, I learned that playing politics is a tricky game. Due to so many different personalities and agendas, politics can definitely be overthought. One must remember that a win is a win, even if it is only by one vote.

Immediately, I had to make a decision. Would I support Richie, or would I oppose him? Richie had too much going for him, so I sat down and made a conscious decision. Troop 249 belonged to Richie. I would use my time as an assistant to learn how to be senior patrol leader. The next six months provided me the opportunity to learn exactly what that meant, and exactly what I would do differently. It was a good thing I made that decision because we would need to find strength in our most dangerous situation yet.

CHAPTER 9
STRANDED

SITTING NEARLY 200 MILES from the Las Vegas valley, due north of the rugged beauty of Utah's Zion National Park, Camp Del Webb was a well-known summer camp destination for Boy Scout troops. Cars, vans, and buses full of scouts, troop leaders, and volunteers made the drive to southern Utah each summer. They wound their way along I-15 through the arid desert, the Virgin River Gorge, and the small town of St. George, Utah. They then traveled along the lonely winding roads through the wild mountains, crevasses, and valleys of Zion National Park, all just to spend a week camping at Camp Del Webb.

A few weeks prior to the camp, the local council asked a band of scouts to prepare Camp Del Webb ahead of time. When the opportunity presented itself to Troop 249, we jumped at the chance. Attending an unprepared campsite meant there would be a higher safety risk though. Thus, the Camp Del Webb preparation experience belonged to the scoutmasters and the more experienced scouts only.

About twelve individuals made up of both scouts and adults accepted the journey. Half of us were from Troop 249, and the other half were adults. While most of the adults had scouting experience, two or three of them were not involved in scouts. They merely wanted to go camping for a long weekend and have an adventure.

Nearing our destination, our small caravan traveled carefully through the winding forested roads between the canyons, the shadows of nature making their presence felt through the side windows.

As I sat next to Richie and Neil in the back seat of Scoutmaster Chuck's truck, we entertained ourselves with the help of comic books and storytelling.

"Hey," Neil interrupted. "Is it true what I heard about that rollover that killed several scouts on the way to Del Webb?"

We had all heard about the accident and the legend was in our young minds as we made our way past the desert into the forest.

"Yes, that did happen," Chuck said. "Thirty years ago, a truck hauling several scouts in the bed of a pickup had a mechanical failure and went over the cliff when the brakes went out."

"Were there any guardrails?" Neil asked.

"And why would they allow scouts to be in the back of a pickup truck like that?" asked Richie.

"Things were different thirty years ago," replied Chuck. "Nowadays they have guardrails, better vehicles, and systems to try to prevent those things from happening again." He was trying to help us feel at ease, but we all knew better.

I had learned early on that nature has a way of humbling human beings. It does not care about morals, government, religion, or feelings. It only knows respect. As soon as that respect for nature is lost, it will remind us just how powerful and wild it is.

Losing respect may be an innocent mistake on the victim's part. Perhaps he slipped under a rock or drove a little too fast along a winding road. Maybe he stepped on a rattlesnake or he was struck by lightning. So many people don't realize that a small amount of rain could mean a flash flood is coming. They forget that hypothermia could cause such disorientation in the mind of the victim that he loses his sense, before disappearing alone into the wilderness.

We have all thought at one time or another that it cannot happen to us, and we don't need to be careful. Suddenly, without warning, we've fallen victim to nature's power. We've been simple and foolish. Our only hope would be to survive to grow wiser. Unfortunately, many do not survive, leaving the rest of us to learn from their mistakes. Because of this, only the adults and the most experienced scouts were allowed on this trip.

As we drove along the roads, curves forced us to slow to embarrassingly low speeds, but disregarding the turns meant we would risk flying off the road into the valley far below. As we rounded each curve, I silently wondered if this was the curve, the one that caused the accident thirty years ago, or if it was the next one, or the next. Each curve had its own sense of treachery, and just one mishap could end in the same result. Each turn demanded respect.

Reaching the top of the canyon, we exited our vehicles and peered over the canyon cliffs into the valley. A winding dirt road, gutted and cracked with erosion, dropped through the trees, ending somewhere in the valley amidst the woods. Camp Del Webb was somewhere in the valley, and the dirt road was the only way in or out. Loaded with supplies, our vehicles had to make the trip along the road. Russ noticed right away that there were no guardrails, and that the switchbacks would make driving down the side of the canyons difficult, if not treacherous. Jesse, his brother, looked up and exclaimed that as long as there was no rain, it should be safe. Still, the drivers would have to use low gear and take their time.

One by one, the vehicles began their descent, except for one. One adult, not affiliated with the scouts at all, decided to volunteer his time just to spend time outdoors. He made the trip in his black jeep, and parked it at the top of the canyon. A little nervous about driving down the road, he decided to grab his walking stick and backpack, and then hike down the road to the valley below, leaving his jeep parked alone, unguarded above the canyon rim.

As he walked, the rest of us sat uncomfortably in our seats. Scoutmaster Chuck's truck bounced and weaved down the road as each tire fell into the eroded soil underneath. Chuck steered as best he could, avoiding the wall above and the cliff below. On more than one occasion, we held our breath as we rounded a switchback. The turn radius was tight, and a wrong bounce could end in our rolling through the trees to a fiery crash several hundred feet down the canyon walls.

At last, we safely reached the valley floor. Camp Del Webb appeared between the trees before us, a collection of wooden structures, picnic tables, and campsites. As we exited our vehicles, I surveyed all that was before me. I had a feeling one gets when they discover they are the only ones at a theme park. Though hundreds of boys would attend Camp Del Webb during the summer, we had exclusive access to experience all the camp had to offer.

The day was perfect. The sun was shining and there wasn't a cloud in the sky or a hint of rain. When we arrived at the campsite, we unloaded the cars, set up our tents, and prepared our campsite. Afterwards, we did what we'd come to do; use our scouting skills to prepare campsites and stations along the canyon that would be used for merit badge lessons, opportunities, and advancement. We picked a large pond down the canyon for lessons in canoeing, swimming, and boating. We picked a clearing further down for compass work while we established a second clearing for archery and rifle shooting. Woodcarving and knot tying were easy to set up, as was first aid. We scheduled camp preparations to take about three days. Little did we know nature had other plans.

In the Pacific Ocean, a tropical storm had made its way along the Gulf of California. Local weather reports sounded no alarm prior to our leaving. However, unbeknownst to us, the storm had worsened into an intense Tropical Depression, which had switched directions, heading straight towards southern California. Two days after we left, the storm flooded the Las Vegas valley and then followed us into the mountains of southern Utah.

The first raindrops did not seem like much as we neared completion of the camp work. However, with a few more hours to go the rain fell upon us with a vengeance. We halted our work, and we focused on keeping our supplies and ourselves dry. The rain continued through the night and we knew our goal of leaving the next morning was lost. We would have to stay longer to finish and we expected to be home later than planned the next day. That night as the rain beat down upon my tent I had a suspicious feeling that we would not get out the next day after all.

The next morning we awoke to a thick fog and a campsite so wet we had to pull our feet forcefully from the mud as we walked. Unfortunately the dirt road back up the canyon was just as muddied, and the adults said there was no way to get our vehicles back up the canyon without risking sliding off the road and down the canyon walls. Our only option was to wait it out and hope the sun would dry the road enough for us to leave the following day.

While the rain held off, we completed our work, and then broke for lunch, hoping the area would dry enough to let us leave. Unfortunately, the reprieve from the rain was brief. Another torrential downpour hit and lasted well into the night. We were low on food and water and no one had a dry piece of clothing to spare.

"If I'm ever in Utah again I'm bringing an extra set of shoes," I thought, as my feet aired out and I hung whatever socks I had out to dry under our tarp.

"How are we going to let our families know that we're ok?" asked Neil the following day. Many were getting concerned their families were worried and wondered how to make contact. We were supposed to return twenty-four hours ago, and we imagined them at home watching their televisions to see if there was any sort of news announcing we were safe. Richie, Josh, Kevin, Russel, and Jesse had come with their fathers, but both Neil and I were there without family. We all hoped a park ranger would send a helicopter out looking for us.

Time traveled slowly and soon we'd been at Camp Del Webb two days longer than planned. We had eaten all of our food and had to borrow from the provisions we'd brought for the summer camps. The rain had dissipated, but the threat from the clouds still hung low in the sky. We needed to send a message letting our families know we were okay, but we were not sure how to make that happen.

Finally, Mike, the volunteer who had walked down from the top of the canyon had an answer. "I still have my jeep up at the top of the mountain. Since the rain has stopped, a few of the boys and I can hike up to the jeep and at least make it back to Vegas. Then we can let everyone know the rest of you are alright and that you're only waiting for the road to dry out enough for you to make it out of the canyon."

The storm had soaked the area so deeply it would likely be another day or two before the cars could make it back up. We decided Mike's idea was our best option and Scoutmaster Chuck determined that since both Neil's and my parents were at home waiting, it was best for us to make the hike with Mike. He also decided to send Scoutmaster Dan's son, Kevin, since Dan's wife was home alone. We imagined she was worried also.

Scoutmaster Chuck asked me, "Matt, would you call my wife when you get in to let her know we're ok?"

"You got it!" I said.

We had to attempt the trip, so as soon as the morning rain stopped, we packed our wet gear as best we could and readied for our trip up the canyon. The only things somewhat dry I had to wear were a flannel shirt and a pair of Bermuda shorts. Mud covered my shoes and socks, and my Australian cowboy hat, which I brought along, was soaked from the rain. It would not be fun lugging wet clothing and supplies on our backs two miles uphill. The mud would make the trip harder and add additional time. We planned conservatively, knowing our supplies were limited and we needed to conserve our energy.

We made the hike up the canyon in three hours. Exhausted but ecstatic to see Mike's black jeep along the ridge Kevin exclaimed, "There it is. Finally!" and we dropped our gear and took a well-deserved break. Beyond the ridge, we saw the wild of the canyon and the weather of southern Utah. The storm was pushing off to the East, and while those below us hoped that the sun would come out and stay out long enough to dry the road, the rest of us were relieved we could begin the five-hour journey to Las Vegas. I imagined that by seven or eight that night, I would be clean and resting in the comfort of home.

The drive through the mountains was a quiet one and there was an air of relief in the car. St. George was close by, and soon we would all have a hot meal. We stopped at a fast food joint, and the other diners stared at us when they saw our condition. We must have looked a sight with our clothes worn and dirty, but we didn't care. Food was all we really wanted. We ate quietly amidst the stares of other patrons before we continued our journey in Mike's jeep towards the setting sun.

The I-15 highway continued towards the Virgin Gorge, and yellow signs warning of falling rocks popped up below the cliffs. As we looked up to see whether there were any threats from above, we couldn't help but realize we'd once again left civilization behind us. We would have to travel through the Gorge and across the Arizona desert into the night before we would see the lights of the small town of Mesquite, Nevada. Still, as we exited the Gorge into the desert, we knew after just a few more hours under the stars we'd be home.

Suddenly, a loud "clunk!" startled us. Steam seeped out from under the jeep's hood. The heavy, bitter scent of something burning filled our noses and throats. The jeep's temperature gauge read hot, so Mike pulled over quickly. A quick check under the hood showed us the fan belt had snapped and, devoid of water, there was nothing to keep the engine cool, which then caused it to burn up.

"After all we've been through," said Neil, "now this!" I shared his frustration. Stranded in the Arizona desert, I looked around to see if there was somewhere we could walk to get help. The Virgin Mountains loomed in the darkness behind us, and the stars above us hung over the darkening valley. The black emptiness of the desert stretched for miles, and I wondered if we would ever find help.

"We'll just have to deal with it," said Mike.

"What are we going to do?" asked Kevin.

"We need a new fan belt," said Mike. "There's probably a fan belt in St. George, but whoever sells them probably won't be open until tomorrow morning. I have some friends who own a shop in Las Vegas, but they will have to wake up, go to their store and get the belt, and then drive the two hours past us to St. George. Then they'd have to come south back along I-15 to bring it to us."

"Ok," I said. "That means we will have to flag down some help."

"Or wait for a police officer to drive by."

"What choice do we have?" said Neil. "Let's start waving!"

As we stood there on the side of the road, we began to wave for help from the trucks that came by in the night. We spotted them coming from a long ways away, but we quickly surmised that they could not see us in time to slow down as they drove by. They drove past us at seventy miles per hour, hitting us with a rush of sound and wind that knocked us backward. More than once, a gust of wind blew my hat off when one of them sped past along the highway.

As one semi neared, a sudden flash of light from the top of his cab blinded us. The light angled so the trucker could see precisely what was on the side of the road. As he drove past, Kevin said, "Are you kidding me? Are they looking at us to see who we are before they offer help?"

"Maybe we need to pretend we're wearing skirts," said Neil. They laughed a nervous laugh, realizing that a stranger could only help our situation. An hour had already gone by, as had several truckers, and we were desperate to get one to pull over so we could radio for help. Whatever we did, no one showed any interest in assisting. We sat on the side of the road for several hours into the night, waving at passersby to no avail until finally a highway patrol officer pulled up behind us.

When Mike showed the patrol officer the broken fan belt, the patrol officer said, "All of the shops in St. George are closed. I don't know if we can get a new fan belt to you from there."

"I figured," said Mike. "But, I have friends who own an auto shop in Vegas. Could I give you their number, so you can call them from St. George? Maybe they can help?"

"They must be good friends," said the highway patrol officer.

"I sure hope they are," said Mike.

We boys glanced at each other. "Great! We're going to be out here all night!" said Neil.

"Maybe, but it's all we have at the moment," I said.

The patrol officer left to head south. About ten minutes later, we saw him heading towards the Gorge to get to his station in St. George. All we could do was hope he could make contact with Mike's friends, and wait.

Less than an hour later, the same highway patrol officer pulled back behind us. "I called and woke up your friends," the patrolman said. "They are going to their store to get a fan belt, and they'll be heading up this way by about now."

"Hooray!" said Neil and Kevin.

"That's good," said Mike. "It'll take about two hours to get to us, but at least we'll get home."

"That means we'll get home around 3:30 in the morning," said Neil.

"Hey, home is home," said Kevin, "as long as we get there." The patrolman left us on the side of the road, and we waited the next few hours for Mike's friends. There were no books, video games, or anything else for that matter to keep us entertained. All we had were the shadows of the mountains in the distance, the stars above, and the rush of wind from the passing tractor-trailers. Every now and again, a trucker flashed his truck light at us as he drove by, but gave no indication that he would stop to help.

Mike's friends finally arrived. They quickly strapped on a new fan belt, poured water into the engine, and started the jeep's engine. Exhausted, we climbed into the jeep and drove south along I-15 towards Las Vegas. A short while later I noticed the glow from the Las Vegas lights illuminating the mountains. Not long after that, we entered the city. The rain that had hit us in Utah had also hit the city. The rainwater had dangerously filled the potholes and the gutters leaving flooded roads and gullies. Those on the streets drove far more cautiously than normal. I realized then that the storm had affected everyone, not just those of us lost in Utah.

I noticed the first hints of dawn when we finally made it to my driveway. I thanked Mike, a man I would never meet again, but who was responsible in a trying situation. My parents were relieved when I found my way inside, and Scoutmaster Chuck's wife was not upset that I woke her up to let her know that he and Richie were doing fine.

After putting my things away and cleaning up, I sat for a few moments on the sofa to reflect upon our adventure. People I knew and did not know had banded together to help one another in a difficult situation. I realized in this storm was a very valuable lesson. When disaster strikes, it's necessary to lean on and support those who are near us, whether we know them or not. There are no allegiances or factions during a tragedy or a disaster. It's important to band together to find a solution and help each other. Trusting in strangers may be difficult, but it could be all we have.

A little over a year later, Richie and I would attend the funerals of three Las Vegas area scouts who were in a bus crash on the way to Camp Del Webb. The camp closed for a time afterwards until officials made further safety precautions. Gladly, no additional tragedies have happened since.

We all face the reality of nature. Many will proclaim that people should stay home because the world is too dangerous, but that is not the right approach. We should not fear nature, but we should respect it. We should also respect and trust each other. Unfortunately, for one reason or another, our leaders do not always have this respect. They misbehave, ignore their responsibilities, and divide us with their poor example. As I soon learned, it takes courage to speak out against poor leaders and their attitudes. Often, that courage is needed when we least expect it.

CHAPTER 10
FACING THE MOB

LATER THAT SUMMER, a new assistant scoutmaster joined our troop. Introducing himself as Assistant Scoutmaster Steve, he stood six feet-eight inches tall. We immediately asked if he was a basketball player. Showing a big grin, he explained in a deep voice that he had no athletic skills of which to brag. His field was engineering and computers. More importantly, he said he wanted to help others. Having recently moved to the Las Vegas area, he decided joining our troop would give him that opportunity. He was big, tall, and goofy, but I liked him instantly. I immediately felt his heart was in the right place.

Richie, on the other hand, seemed ready to relinquish his senior patrol leader position. I wondered how I would do things differently as I watched him exercise authority over the boys. I wondered if I, too, would be frustrated. When elections returned that fall, Richie announced he was not going to run again. Feeling ready, I decided I had prepared well the past six months and I announced my decision to run. Though I had no opposition, the scoutmasters passed around paper ballots. Even though this time I knew for certain I would win, I made sure to put my name on the ballot. Scoutmaster Chuck announced my victory to the troop, and upon acceptance, I asked Richie to be my assistant, as I had originally planned. He accepted, so we would lead Troop 249 together again.

I was somewhat surprised when Scoutmaster Chuck also stepped down as the head scoutmaster a few weeks later. Choosing to remain an assistant, Chuck relinquished the position to Scoutmaster Steve. Steve had only been with us a couple of months, but he had obviously made an impression with the troop council. The new leadership would bring the winds of change to Troop 249. Understanding this one evening in my room, I said a prayer for God to help me with my new responsibility, and I sat down with a pen and paper to plot our course.

Scoutmaster Steve and I formed a quick bond. With both of us being new to our roles, we felt the troop's success depended on our ability to work together. He offered great direction in organizing the troop. We decided to take rank advancement and outdoor experiences to an even higher level, and he let me take the lead in how to do it. For the following summer camp, we decided to take on Lake Arrowhead. Whereas our previous summer camps entertained a few hundred boys, Lake Arrowhead in California held close to a thousand campers. I wanted to build our reputation across the southwest United States, and making a name for ourselves in the heavily attended Lake Arrowhead gave us a great opportunity to do just that.

When the time for camp came, we did what we had always done at arrival; we set up our camp space first and then organized the boys for their merit badge classes the following day. Merit badges were crucial to rank advancement, and I held a troop meeting explaining how everyone's part was important to the troop's success. My troop gathered enthusiastically, but as I spoke I noticed how our boys swatted at oncoming mosquitos, and I wondered whether they heard me or if the elements kept them too distracted.

As we were gathered, a camp staff member walked towards us. About to turn twenty, he told us that most of staff members were about the same age. The staffers, as we called them, spent several weeks at Lake Arrowhead helping run the camp. His task on this visit was to make sure we knew where important amenities were, such as the main office, the showers, the infirmary, and the dining hall. We thanked him for his help, and said our goodbyes.

As the staffer was leaving, he turned and asked, "By the way, who among you is the senior patrol leader?"

I looked up and said, "That would be me. Why do you ask?"

"We have a council of senior patrol leaders that you'll need to attend. You're all going to get together and decide how you're going to make this camp week special."

"Sounds good," I said. "I'll be there." As he walked away, I wondered exactly what he was saying. What were we going to do? How do we decide what direction to go? I felt excited to be in the midst of other senior patrol leaders and to compare myself to them. I hoped it would be an opportunity to build Troop 249's reputation among the southwest.

The following afternoon, after my merit badge classes ended, I arrived at the senior patrol leader council. A light drizzle had cooled the afternoon air, and around thirty of us gathered under a large blue tarp formed into a tent near the dining hall. I looked at the other boys and I thought it was an impressive group. Most of the senior patrol leaders had mid-to-advanced ranks and were older than many of the other scouts at camp.

Amidst the small talk, I felt an interesting presence among the group. These young men shared the experience of leading others.

We talked amongst ourselves until two staffers, each wearing their red Lake Arrowhead staff shirts, arrived and joined us in the conversation.

"Here they are. What a good group of leaders we have here!" said the smaller staffer. He introduced himself, and we in turn said our hellos and made introductions.

"So, what are we going to do to make this camp special?" said the other, larger staffer.

After a briefly uncomfortable pause I asked, "Well, what do people usually do? I'm sure you've seen a lot of things."

"Good question. I can tell you that the end of camp always ends with a big campfire, and we'll have to plan that. However, we also want to do something else, and that'll be up to all of you."

"Ok," I said. I was surprised no one else really spoke up, so I kept going. "How about if we have a competitive obstacle course?"

"An obstacle course?" said a senior patrol leader on my right. "What do you have in mind?"

"You know, something we can all be a part of. We will use the entire camp area, and we'll have all sorts of competitions around at several stations. It'll be like a relay race. Each of the troops can dedicate one of their members to each station, and at the end whoever performs as the best team will get an award at the campfire at the end of the week."

One of the staff members said, "Will you be in charge of it?"

"Sure," I said. "In fact, we'll do both the obstacle course and the campfire ceremonies."

"Sounds good to me," said one of the other senior patrol leaders on my left. I saw that he was happy he did not have to take on any additional responsibility.

"Ok then," said the staff member. "You draw out your plans, and we'll meet back here tomorrow to narrow down the details."

"You got it," I said.

"Well, that was quick," said another senior patrol leader. We quickly disbursed, and I returned to our campsite.

"Gather around," I said to my troop. "We have some things coming up that you all need to know about." Everyone formed around me in a small semi-circle. "First, we're going to have an obstacle course near the end of the week."

"Will I get to run?!" said Sean excitedly.

"Yes, you'll get to run," I said. "In fact, everyone is going to have something to do. The other senior patrol leaders and I are going to run the obstacle course, but as for Troop 249, we're all going to work together to win this thing."

"Awesome!" said Robby.

"One more thing," I said. "We're also responsible for the closing ceremonies at the last campfire. We need to come up with a skit, and I'm going to need help organizing that."

"You signed us up for both?" asked Scoutmaster Steve.

"I did. Are you ok with that?"

Steve nodded his head and said, "Yeah. That's a lot, but let us know if you need help handling it."

"We'll be fine," I said, and I began delegating tasks amongst the troop.

…

The day of the race was exciting. Anticipation had been building all week, and the boys did a great job at organizing the entire event. Sean, our resident sprinter, opted to go first. The course, however, did not begin with a sprint; it began with a hardboiled egg-eating contest. Knowing that egg-eating contests didn't typically turn out well, I was surprised he had agreed to start.

When Sean ran to the next leg, Kory executed his Frisbee throwing expertise at his station, and the race continued. Richie shot the target with his rifle. Robbie hit his target with his arrows. Neil tied his rope into knots as fast as he could. Jesse worked his compass magic.

Kevin and Russ ran their three-legged race. Josh did his potato sack race, and then he sprinted towards the finish line.

Another very large troop from southern California also competed well. With Troop 249 from Nevada doing so well, it seemed that the competition was not among the troops, but between the states. The boys from California cheered for their home state, while our Nevada boys did everything we could to win.

In the end, Troop 249 finished a close second behind the large California troop. We weren't the largest troop at the camp, but we worked well together, and that didn't go unnoticed. Other troops commended us on our teamwork and efforts. Our team from Las Vegas had earned recognition, and I smiled as I let each of our players know how proud I was of them.

…

The closing ceremonies had arrived. As the sun set behind us in the western sky, a thousand scouts and their scoutmasters sat in the amphitheater. Front and center, a roaring fire danced, throwing orange and red hues towards all the attendees. As all the troops had done, Troop 249 prepared a skit most of the afternoon. Taking only a minor role in the skit, I stepped away a time or two to prepare for my other duty as Master of Ceremonies. With a starry sky above, I stepped onto the stage and faced the audience.

"Thank you all for a great week of camp!" I began. "We've had a wonderful time here, and to get things started off, allow me to introduce my troop, Troop 249 from Las Vegas, NV. We're from the entertainment capital of the world, so without any undue pressure, let's begin this thing right!" I looked to my left at my troop aligned next to me. "Take it, boys!"

One by one, each troop performed their act in front of the audience. Most acts were humorous, some were off color, but I did not concern myself with what was happening on stage so much as I was making sure the action behind the scene was in rhythm.

Unfortunately, I never thought to look to see what was happening with the audience.

Suddenly, two of the camp staffers appeared in front of me with very concerned look on their faces. "You've got to do something," one of them said to me.

"What do you mean? What's going on?" I asked.

"The crowd is getting out of control," the other said. "It's bad."

"Really?" I asked. I turned around. On the stage, a small troop was singing their version of "In the Jungle" as sung by The Tokens, but then my eyes turned towards the crowd, and I was horrified. I watched in dismay as several adult scoutmasters and their troops heckled the performers. They booed, laughed, and pointed, their behavior out of control. My jaw dropped when I saw one adult stand from his seat shouting, "Sit down! You're awful!" The audience had become an uncontrollable mob, and as the performing boys halted their song and angrily walked off the stage, I marched to the center to face the mob alone.

A fierce emotion welled up inside me as I quietly stood on center stage. I looked those adult leaders who made me the most disappointed directly in the eyes. I raised my right hand in the traditional Boy Scout sign with three fingers pointed at the stars above. I did not move. The loud noises quieted to a whisper as the thousand scouts and the adults began to notice me on stage. Even when the night became silent save for the crackling of the fire, I stood for several long moments eyeing the worst culprits, just to let them know I was in control.

"What are we doing?" I asked as I lowered my hand. "Is this what we're all about? We spend a week together building each other up, and then we lose it all at the end by tearing each other apart? This is embarrassing. What do we stand for if this is how we act?" I let a few moments go by as they pondered in the silence. "And, you adults," I began again, "what example are you trying to show your troops? Is this how you behave? We look to you for leadership and for example. Is this really the example you want to set?"

I asked the troop that had left the stage if they wanted to continue their performance, but they chose not to. The night was still young, and the show had to go on, but I was apprehensive about continuing.

I took a deep breath and said, "So, we have half the troops still to perform their entertainment for tonight. We have a choice as to how we end the ceremonies. How will you decide? Will we build each other up, or will we not?" I turned around, and went to the next troop on deck where I said to them, "Not an easy way to get going, but you guys have a skit to do, and I want you to do your best. Are you ready?"

"We are," said one of the performers.

"Great!" I said. "Go out there and break a leg! Not literally, of course! I definitely don't want that on my conscience tonight." They chuckled as they walked past me onto the stage. I looked at the two staffers next to me. Neither said a word. Their worried faces now expressed astonishment. I said nothing to them. I turned briefly to watch the audience clap with appreciation at the performance on the stage. Sensing the mob defeated, I turned and once again prepared the next troop behind the curtain.

I think many of us learned several important lessons that night. First, we need to support and respect each other, and I am hopeful that those in attendance that night carry this thought with them still.

Second, it is impossible to have an awareness of everything. We need to rely on our team to help alert us when there is a concern, such as witnessing a crowd getting out of hand. Had the camp staffers not alerted me, it could have gotten far worse. I only wished they had alerted me sooner.

Third, I learned that influencers must make the decision to lead or be a part of the crowd. Those in a leadership position wield a great opportunity to bring others to goodness, or drag their followers down to the depths of inhumaneness. Adult influencers who forget their positions and succumb to weakness direct tomorrow's leaders along the path of brokenness and anarchy.

Finally, I realized that the one who has the podium has great authority, even at a young age. At fourteen, my stance at the prominent position in front of the crowd afforded me the opportunity to quiet a situation gone awry. By standing on truth, and reminding them of virtue, I was able to bring the crowd back to the right place. I had a message, and the message made the difference.

In that moment, I led a large crowd to behave with respect and kindness. My hope was not to ridicule, but to bring back those who were lost. I wonder these days if the members of that audience remember that night, and whether or not they carry that message with them. Whether they do or not, I know today that leaders choose to make a difference in the lives of those they serve.

After that night, I felt I was ready for the next step. Though most scouts waited until they were much older to start their Eagle Project, I realized that the time had arrived for me to begin mine. I returned home with my Life rank, and a drive within me to bring others together to discover how we might change the world.

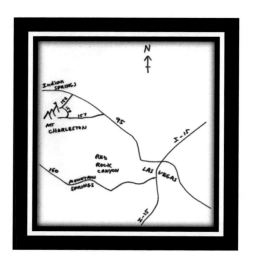

CHAPTER 11
THE FENCE

EVERY SCOUT MUST COMPLETE A PROJECT if he wants to get his Eagle. We often discussed ideas with each other regarding our projects, such as what they would look like or when we would get to them; yet many scouts never completed their project. Many times a boy would get busy in high school with sports or girlfriends and drop out before completing his project, just like the scoutmaster I had met at the Jamboree. Sometimes a scout would miss the age deadline, and he would never make the rank of Eagle, though he gave it his best effort. There were times when a scout would submit a project idea, but the council would reject it and the scout would have to go back to the drawing board until he submitted an acceptable idea.

Our troop council was meticulous about the projects they approved. We had high standards and, if a project did not meet those standards, the project was not accepted. Life outside of the Boy

Scouts was busy enough with school, sports, jobs, and social activities. The troop council required meticulous preparation, which made the project task even more difficult.

As the senior patrol leader, I thrived on watching each scout grow as a person through the scout experience. Doing so, however, forced me to push the troop to new heights.

Literally.

There were four mountains in particular around the southwest that attracted our attention, and our troop decided we needed to conquer each of them. Those four mountains were Mount Charleston, Mount Potosi, Sunrise Mountain, and Mount Baldy.

Mount Charleston was closest, and to the northwest of the Las Vegas Valley. Mount Potosi was to the southwest, just next to the canyons of Red Rock. Sunrise Mountain dawned under the eastern sunrise, and far beyond, hundreds of miles away in New Mexico, stood Mount Baldy at Camp Philmont.

If we were to continue with our reputation, Troop 249 had to conquer Mount Baldy. With tremendous focus, it would take months of planning and preparation, along with practice runs up nearby mountains. Because this was important to the troop, working on my own project seemed self-serving. The troop meant more to me at that moment, but the rank of Eagle required the project. If I was to advance the troop and set the example for others, I decided it was best to complete my project immediately after I became a Life Scout. There could be no waiting. Once done, I would then be free to get back to work on the troop. Moreover, with the recent experience I just had at Lake Arrowhead, I felt I was ready.

So, what would my project be? At first, I had no idea. I knew it had to be community oriented, have a government component and not benefit someone's personal property. Of course, it had to be legal, but nothing came to mind.

My father had also earned the rank of Eagle Scout in his day, so I went to him. "Dad," I asked. "What did you do for your Eagle project?"

"Not much," he said. "About four or five of us dug a hole and put a road sign in the ground."

"That's it?!" I asked.

"Pretty much," he said.

There was no way my council would accept a project as simple as that, I thought. Anything our council accepted would need a good reason behind the project, a story. It needed something that invoked passion, and that, when completed, would help many people. I also knew the council would want something big enough for the entire troop to participate in.

The only person I knew in a government role was Forest Ranger Don at Mount Charleston. My mother and I had met him and his family while exploring the mountain shortly after moving to Las Vegas.

"Mom," I said. "Can we call Forest Ranger Don? Maybe he has an idea for an Eagle Project."

"Sure," she said, and she picked up the phone. Don did have an idea, however, it was a big one and he suggested my mother and I drive up to Mount Charleston to understand the full scope of the project.

The following weekend, Don took us to the Mount Charleston canyons. "There it is," he said. He pointed to the mountainside with large trees blanketing the western slope. "People use this slope to sled down every winter when it snows, and there are so many of them it's hard to stop them. Unfortunately, one girl was sledding down the slope last winter and ran head first into that tree over there. She died instantly with a broken neck. We don't want to see that happen again, and we need to stop them somehow."

"What are you proposing?" I asked.

"Two fences," he suggested. "If we build two fences along the face of the slope, people won't have a slope to sled down."

"That makes sense," I said.

"They have to be real long, though. The slope stretches over several hundred feet. With our budget cuts, we just can't hire the labor to get it done. We could sure use a good sized team to help us with it."

"I think we can manage that. We have a large troop, and if needed I can recruit more people to help. If you can just provide the wood and the materials, I think we can bring the tools and the people."

"Perfect," said Don. "Let's coordinate next week."

There were many details to cover. I needed to know the type of wood, how much we would need, the dimensions, weight, color, cost, when it would be available, and how they would all arrive at the work site.

I would need to know exactly where they'd want the fence built, why they chose that specific lumber, and why they did not choose a different lumber type. Why did they choose a fence as the structure to achieve the objective? Why not some other structure?

I would need to explain in my paperwork the types of tools we would need, and why the project required certain tools over others. I would have to determine what we would borrow or purchase, and how we would get them to and from the mountain. If we would have to purchase them, I'd have to organize another event, a fundraiser, to raise the money to purchase the tools. I would have to determine manpower and the tasks as well as who would perform each task to get the job done. Given the size of the project, I had regretted not asking to just dig a hole and stick a sign in it.

I needed to provide a complete plan of action, touching on every single point from project preparation to its completion. The council would need all of the details and I worried I wouldn't be able to provide enough. The planning exercise had me thinking of every possible scenario and detailing an execution process on paper. As tedious as it was, it worked.

With several people working on that mountain, we organized well enough that everyone involved managed to help in some way or another. The moms handled the first aid and food, while dads, scouts, and my friend Travis dug the stake holes. My father, teaching me the valuable lesson of working smarter and not harder, rented a post hold digger to speed up the entire process, helping us finish in one day instead of the two I had originally planned.

However, I had an issue with their instruction preventing me from doing any of the physical labor. One troop councilwoman reminded me often not to touch anything. I picked up a wrench or a shovel to work on one of the posts, but Scoutmaster Steve caught me and took it away from me. He told me that my job was to oversee everyone and to not get caught up in the details. "Not get caught up in the details!" I said. "Do you realize how many details I had to figure out to get us here? I'd feel good just digging one hole after all the work I've done."

"Can't let you do it," said Steve.

"This is crazy!" I said, and I turned to oversee and encourage the other scouts who were digging holes and fixing nuts and bolts.

Nearing the end of the day, we had two rows of fence along the slope of Mount Charleston. Before the last bolt was set, everyone gathered next to it and called me towards them.

"Where's Matt?" asked Scoutmaster Steve. My troop, family, and friends stood in a tight circle next to him. They all looked tired, but they also knew they had accomplished a great task.

"I'm right here," I said.

"Well, we have one last bolt to tighten, and we think it would be appropriate if you finish it."

"Really? So now I can actually tighten a bolt?"

He handed me a wrench. "It's all yours."

I stood in the middle of the volunteers and twisted the wrench to make the bolt tight. When I finished, I raised my arms triumphantly and the whole group cheered a mighty, "Hooray!" I still had to write up a detailed post-operative paper on the final outcome, and I had to give it to the council for approval.

However, the physical labor was done, and several hundred feet of wooden fencing had been erected along the mountainside, deterring would be snow adventurers from crashing into trees and risking their lives. The wooden fence would stand for several years, succeeding in its mission. Years of weather, however, would wear it down, and officials would later replace the fence with a more stable rod-iron structure with the same purpose.

Nevertheless, on that late afternoon, before we gathered our belongings to head down to the valley below, I ran my fingers over the wooden railing and sensed something over my shoulder. I felt a chill from the shadow that came from the western ridge. Night was coming, and with it the cool mountain air. High above, I could see the faint snow-covered heights of the Mount Charleston Peak. Something up there called to me. I felt a premonition that next summer we would challenge the mountain that looked down upon us from the evening sky.

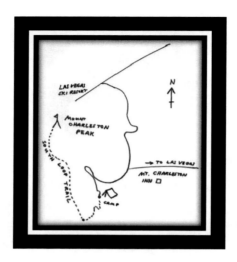

CHAPTER 12
CLIMBING THE MOUNTAIN

MOUNT CHARLESTON OVERLOOKS the Las Vegas Valley approximately thirty-five miles to the west. Each evening at dusk, the residents can watch the sunset as it drifts beyond the ridge, leaving the shadow of the peak as a reminder of the disappearance of day, and an early opportunity for the Las Vegas lights to begin their nightly battle against the moon and stars above.

The Mount Charleston Peak stands at just less than 12,000 feet above sea level. We thought it best to complete a peak that high in stages. Because of its monumental size, it was not something we wanted to climb in one day. Instead, we chose to camp above the Mount Charleston Lodge, pack up and eat breakfast early the next morning, and climb among all the switchbacks to get to the mountainous ridge.

The ridge, called the South Loop Trail, would be our first high endurance test. While several younger scouts declined the adventure, every one of our more experienced scouts made the trip. As for myself, I imagined often during sunsets the prospect of conquering the Mount Charleston Peak as it cast its shadow over the valley. Knowing I could say, "I was up there," drove inside me the need to reach the top, and there was no way I would miss the chance.

Several scoutmasters and fathers decided to help us. Excitement filled the mountain air as we awoke from our tents, packed our gear into the trucks, and headed along the base of the trail. Some of the fathers, knowing the difficulty we would endure, offered to stay behind on watch patrol, making sure our belongings were safe for our return later that evening. The rest of us packed our water bottles, first-aid kits, and sunscreen. Many of us brought with us walking sticks for additional balance. I shifted in my hiking boots to feel if they were fitting properly. It really wouldn't matter though, I thought. I'm going to get a blister somewhere on my feet for this one. Just get ready to work through it.

As the cool morning air enveloped us, the June desert below would heat up to above one hundred degrees. However, up here in this high elevation, the air was crisp. I saw the faint hint of smog drifting towards us in the eastern light. It stretched like a tentacle, but unable to permeate the beauty of the fresh air around us.

"Steve, are we ready," I asked. Scoutmaster Steve, donning his cap, strapped on his backpack and grasped his walking stick. Underneath his glasses and his lengthy six-foot-eight frame, Steve possessed such an enjoyment for the outdoors and an enthusiasm for adventure that it was hard not to let his spirit rub off on you.

"I'm ready," he said in his deep voice. "Are all of you?"

"Might as well get going," said Richie.

"Ready or not, here we come," said Neil.

Saying goodbye to those watching the vehicles, we looked up along the side of the mountain. The first half of the trail was nothing but a march up multiple switchbacks to get to the mountain's ridge.

Each step became more difficult as we hit higher altitude. It appeared we would need to stop to catch our breath regularly. One father experienced some dizziness about halfway up. "Guys, I think I'm getting altitude sickness," he said.

"What do you want to do?" asked Assistant Scoutmaster Dan.

"I don't want you guys to not make it on account of me," he said, "but I've got to go back down this mountain."

"Will you be alright," said Steve.

"I'll be fine. You guys go on ahead. I'll watch the gear with the other guys down below." He turned and walked back the other way. I was a little surprised at how quickly he made his decision. As I watched him walk down the mountain, I realized the size of the task at hand. It would not be easy to climb this mountain. It would test our will, but if we put one foot in front of the other and focused on our goal, we could do it.

An hour or so later, we came to a clearing. Fir trees and grassy meadows donned the mountain ridge. Everything was clear along the trail to the north. Large mounds of white snowdrifts, snow from the previous winter that had never melted, shone in the sun under the clear blue sky.

Across the western horizon, we saw another valley, a barren desert until the next mountain ridge in the far off distance. I thought how unusual that Mount Charleston, as big as it was, stood all alone from other mountains in the region. What long ago geographical occurrence caused this rock to climb as high as it did in the middle of an ancient sea? Had it once been a volcano? Did an earthquake raise it from the depths?

"It looks like we have another four and a half miles to go," said Richie. I then noticed the sign pointing the way north along the South Loop Trail. The Peak was somewhere off in the distance, and we figured we'd get there by early afternoon.

"Well, we might as well get going," I said, "if we want to make it off this mountain before nightfall."

We hiked along the ridge amidst the firs and mounds of snow. Though the trail became more level, the higher altitude forced us to take our time. I noticed the first sign of heat coming from my right shoe. A blister, I thought. That's ok. I'll get through it.

During our next break, I sat down, took off my shoe, and grabbed a Band-Aid from my first aid kit. As I doctored my foot, I watched my troop. Weariness had set in, and I could see the first hints of discouragement. Fearing disappointment, I put my shoe back on and jumped up. "Let's get going!" I said. "I think I can see the top from here."

Though the trail elevated slightly, the truth was that the peak was nowhere in sight. We climbed a hill, thinking it would be the peak, only to get to the other side and see another higher peak a few hundred yards away. Peak after peak we climbed, and it was wearing our patience. "How many more of these hills do we have to climb?" said one of the boys.

I didn't say anything. The high altitude and the sun's rays sapped our energy. I heard more and more grumbling with every step. "Where was the end," I thought. We did not know.

Finally, we came upon a steep part of the trail that had a much higher trajectory. "This has got to be the last one," said one of the older boys. We marched slowly with the hope that we had finally reached the summit. Many of us hoped we would soon be finished and then we could begin the return trip down. Sadly, as we reached the heights, we saw the true summit. Off in the distance, about a mile away down an embankment and up a narrow climb stood the peak. I estimated we needed another forty minutes from where we stood just to reach our destination.

Behind me, I heard one of the boys exclaim, "All the way over there?! That's it. I'm not going one more step!"

"Me too! This is crazy!"

"It's not worth it,"

"My feet are killing me,"

"Why did we decide to go on this hike anyway?"

I continued to stand on the hill with my back to my troop, staring at the peak. At that moment, I felt the mountain's challenge. It was personal. Was I going to turn around, too?

Steve stood next to me, the sun glimmering off a pin on his hat. He wiped some sweat off his brow. "Well, Matt," he said. "What do you want to do?"

I didn't look at him. I stared at the trail ahead and said, "I didn't come all this way to not make it to the top."

"Ok," said Steve. "You may want to let the others know what you're going to do."

I turned around. Many of the boys had taken off their shoes, sat on rocks, grumbled about how tough it was, and demanded to turn and head back down. As I looked at them, I realized I had a choice to make.

"Guys," I said. "I'm going to finish this. If I have to do it alone, I will. If all of you want to stay here, you're welcome to. That's your choice. But I didn't come all the way up here to let this mountain beat me. Decide now if you want to change your mind. I'm leaving in five minutes."

Steve said, "I'm coming with you."

"So am I," said Assistant Scoutmaster Dan.

"You know what," said Neil. "I'm coming, too."

"Anybody else coming?" I asked. No one raised his hand.

"You can have it," said one of the boys. "I'm going to sit right here and watch you walk up there."

"Suit yourself," I said. I sat for a few minutes to adjust my shoe. The heat from the blister burned, but I told myself to push through. I looked at Steve, Dan, and Neil. "You guys ready?" I asked.

"Let's go," said Dan, and we turned our backs to the troop and resumed our journey towards the summit.

The hike was tougher than we thought. The elevation pushed us both emotionally and physically, daring us to return to the others. Our breaths became more difficult. We'd have to take more breaks. Every now and again, we'd look back to the troop. We could see them sitting together in the far distance. I focused my gaze on the peak, and thought to myself that we had to keep moving.

We had heard rumors of a small plane that had crashed on the mountain many years before. Unbeknown to us, the crashed plane was the remnant of a secret military flight, carrying several service members. Because government officials kept the flight a secret, the families of the deceased never knew what had happened for several years, and much of the wreckage remained next to the cliffs near the peak. Years later, a memorial in the Mount Charleston Visitor's Center would be erected in the servicemen's honor, along with the propeller from the doomed aircraft on display.

As we neared the peak, we noticed below us the wreckage, its paint weathered and its windows broken. One wing lay several feet from the body. The other wing was missing, probably having fallen off the cliffs below.

At last, with several laborious steps, we reached the summit. I immediately scanned the horizon for it appeared the whole earth was in my view. Off to the east sat the Las Vegas Valley and further east the blue water of Lake Meade. To our north was the wild terrain where the military performed their testing operations. To the west was a desert valley with a variety of mountains intermixed with small desert villages. To the south was the ridge of the South Loop Trail where our troop remained. From where we stood, they seemed like ants in the distance.

Marking the top stood a stand holding a metal box. Opening the box, we found a worn journal and some pens. Inside the journal were handwritten signatures and notes from others who had completed the journey to the peak. We took turns writing our names in the journal. As I signed my name, I realized the magnitude of the moment. Only those who completed the journey received the privilege to be a part of history, and I felt pride for having been there at that moment.

After resting for a while, we returned to our troop. When we joined them, we didn't speak much. It seemed the boys were more concerned with just getting off the mountain.

Suddenly, one boy asked, "Was it there?"

"You mean the plane?" said Neil.

"Yeah, was it there?"

"It was there," Neil said. Neil and I looked at each other. There was not a whole lot else to say, though I thought how I was proud of him for having conquered the mountain.

The return hike to the vehicles went quickly, as return trips often went. When we reached the trucks, we climbed in the cars and began the caravan back to the valley. Along the way, I looked up at the evening sky. Twenty-five of us had begun the journey. Twenty-three of us made it where the end was visible. Yet only four of us reached the summit. It surprised me how quickly and easily so many had decided finishing wasn't worth it, even with our destination immediately before us. What made people want to quit just before they reached the very end?

For me, finishing was an act of will. I often thought how I loved the desert sunsets. I knew that if I did not do all I could to get to the top of that peak, each sunset would haunt me forever for the rest of my life. I'd look west, and I'd remember I gave up. Looking back, I contemplated that thought when I was standing there at that critical moment next to Steve. I had to take the opportunity, and I had to do it then. I could not let the moment slip away.

Maybe the others never had that thought. Maybe the mountain didn't have meaning to them. Maybe that's why so few find success in life. Roughly eighty percent of the people on that hike gave up right before the finish and only twenty percent of us actually reached the goal. Was that really all the difference between success and failure, just a decision to continue a few extra steps?

As we drove down the mountain, the day turned to dusk, and the red and orange sky illuminated the clouds in the eastern sky. A few stars appeared off in the horizon above the faint glow of the Las Vegas lights. Exhausted, I turned briefly to see the last of the sunset disappearing beyond the mountain's peak. I smiled, shut my eyes, and went to sleep.

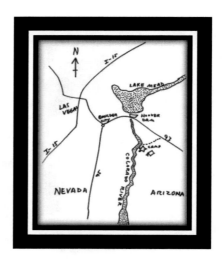

CHAPTER 13
THE CALL

EXCITED TO CAMP ALONG THE BANKS of the Colorado River, I could hardly contain myself as we arrived at our destination. We parked the cars along the road, and looked into the desert. The trail disappeared amidst the sagebrush and the sandy knolls. Though the hike appeared innocent from our vantage point, a potential danger lurked beyond the sagebrush. A groove of rocks and knolls formed deeper along the trail. The further we hiked I noticed how the groove became a ditch, and then became a wash with sixty foot walls. I looked up and I imagined what we would do if danger appeared. My heart beat faster as I concluded that an escape over the limestone walls would be impossible. We could no longer see the horizon, or the sun depending on where it was in the sky. As we felt the coolness of the shade in the wash below, we recognized our only two options. We would have to either finish the trail to the river below, or return the way we came.

A wall of water rushing downhill along the path of gravity created most canyons in the southwest. Because desert sand does not hold water, any significant amount of rain would collect in a gully, head downhill in a ten-foot wall of foam, and form itself into a violent carver of the surrounding geography. Flash floods, as they are called, have taken the lives of many people throughout the years. Many in their cars approached flooded roadways and believed their vehicle protected them. Sadly, authorities would find them in a wash downstream, buried in their flooded car in a watery grave.

Others that were lost resembled us, hikers who braved the trails formed from a violent wall of water. Survivors of those lost in a flash flood told the same story. They heard a rumbling of echoes bouncing along and over the rocks. Many were confused because the sun was shining. Suddenly, a wall of water had appeared around the canyon walls, and in a moment it washed many of them away without a trace. Searchers found their bodies later, buried in the sand at the floor of the canyon walls.

We parked our cars on the Arizona side of the Colorado River. The sky was bright blue in the late afternoon, and the trail would lead us through a wash a few miles down to the campsite, a beautiful location along the edges of the Colorado. Our campsite sat downstream from the Hoover Dam, but far below the heights of the massive canyon walls above. This was to be our first camping trip along the Colorado River.

As we walked into the canyon, the walls around us grew and the shadows darkened. Night came upon us quickly. More so than usual, I thought.

"Where are the stars?" asked one Scout. Curious, we looked up between the walls of the canyon at the blackness. Suddenly, a bright light blinded us and a loud crack of thunder echoed violently between the canyon walls. The hairs on the back of my neck stiffened as pieces of sandstone fell from the walls around us. One of the boys dropped his flashlight. I immediately knew the danger we faced.

"This isn't good," I said.

"What do you mean?" asked one of our newer scouts.

"We're in flash flood territory, and now we have a sudden storm on us."

"We need to hurry," exclaimed Steve.

"Everybody, grab your things and hold tight. We have to run," I shouted. Just as I finished speaking, a second flash and a loud crack of thunder echoed inside the canyon. I looked and saw Josh put his hands above his head as rocks again fell from the cliffs above us.

"Are we going to die?" asked a new scout.

"Not if we run!" I said. "Everybody, let's go!"

We rushed through the darkness as best we could. Every seven or eight seconds, a flash lit the sky above us and a ferocious crack knocked sandstone from the surrounding walls. One of the boys ran into a rock and dropped his flashlight. Another lost his hat when a rock from above struck its brim. As he stopped to look for his hat, another boy grabbed him yelling, "Forget it! We'll get it on the way back!"

The thunder boomed louder, and the lightning flashed in violent bursts, one after another after another. We feared the storm was intent on our destruction. Even though it was not raining on us directly, we knew it was raining somewhere nearby. I could only hope it chose a different canyon to flood. It was as if we were suddenly stuck in a game of Russian Roulette, not knowing which chamber had the greatest danger. Our only chance of protecting ourselves from a flash flood was to get to the Colorado's edge and out from between the canyon walls.

We ran for another twenty minutes, the canyon walls looming larger and larger around us. Finally an opening appeared. We turned right, running to safety away from the mouth of the canyon.

Catching our breath, we set up and staked our tent amidst the lightning and the thunder. We built our fire, and watched the sky above as we waited for the threat to move on.

"Hey, there are the stars again," said Josh. The sky cleared and the bright lights of the stars reflected upon the smooth waters of the Colorado River. No walls of water rushed down our canyon, and, for the first time that night, we felt at ease.

I woke up tired the next morning, the adrenaline from the night before had kept me from sleeping well. The hike itself was moderate, but Troop 249 had expanded, and the new members were young, and inexperienced. For many, this was their first camping trip. I reflected on my first camping trip at the Valley of Fire. That trip was cold and quiet. While I reflected on the danger on the plateau, I compared it to the danger that threatened us last night, and I was thankful we did not wash away into the Colorado River. Our new scouts had definitely come away with a real experience.

After breakfast, we were free to explore. I hung around the campsite and watched the boys climb in and around the rocks along the river. After a few moments, I heard some excitement. Sean ran back to me exclaiming, "There's a sidewinder rattlesnake on those rocks over there!"

"Well, what do you think is the right thing to do with him?" I asked.

"We don't want to get too close, that's for sure!"

"That's right. If you leave him alone, he'll leave you alone. Just go and tell the rest of the gang to go exploring somewhere else, and to be careful where they step."

I watched as Sean ran back to the boys to deliver the message, and I made certain that they moved from the area to explore elsewhere.

"Hey Matt, I've got a question for you," said Scoutmaster Steve. He sat on a small boulder near the fire pit, whittling a stick with his pocketknife. I could tell he was pensive. He had not said much on this trip down the canyon. Even when we were running for our lives, he was rather quiet.

"What's on your mind?"

"Well, I think I'm being called to become a priest."

I paused. Steve and I had become good friends, and I believed we shared a mutual respect, but when he decided to confide in me about something so incredibly personal, I could not help but be surprised.

"I'm not sure what to think of it," he continued, "but I'd like to know your thoughts, and if you think I would be a good one."

I looked away and took in the beauty of the banks of the River. I admired the peacefulness of the water as it slowly made its way between the canyon walls, and I remembered the Sacrament of Baptism. Steve was considering baptized baptism into a new life. Although I was young, I knew our shared respect and friendship had deepened in that instant and what I said next could not only change his life, but potentially the lives of others if he did, in fact, become a priest.

"Steve," I said, "the world can be crazy. Nature can be wild and violent, and men can be more so. The world needs good men who help lead the way. You are a good man. I believe that God is real, and you can't help but realize that when you see the beauty even here on the banks of this river. If He's calling you to be a priest, I think you'd make a very good one. It won't be easy, but He'll prepare you for whatever He needs you to do."

"Thanks, Matt. I appreciate that," he said. As we talked further, I thought of the dangerous hike the night before, and the symbolism was not lost on me. We had survived a dangerous storm, only to find peace after we reached the clearing and the calm waters below. How often are our lives like that? When God makes His offer to us, we don't accept it right away. We struggle. Wrestling with God's offer creates a storm in our lives.

That storm begins internally from the depths of our souls. The more we struggle with His offer, the more we are affected. The struggle affects our relationships, our possessions, our finances, and our lives.

It is only when we accept God's calling that we find true peace. Sometimes that calling is for us to go to a certain place, and sometimes to choose a certain profession, often without regard to profit. While we may not have considered the path, sometimes we have to accept the talents He put inside us, and forego the illusion of being something we are not.

Nevertheless, each time He calls upon us it creates a violent storm, just like the storm above the canyon walls. To find our peace, like the scouts on that hike that night, we simply have to follow the right path. It is then we can experience the quiet baptism from the river below.

CHAPTER 14
ZION

WE BEGAN OUR HIKE early that morning. It was early June, and the sky, a deep blue, outlined the horizon. The landscape resembled one from the late Cretaceous period, and if I had caught a glimpse of a pack of velociraptors hunting a triceratops, it would not have surprised me.

The plan was to prepare the older scouts for Philmont with a hike down a simple fifteen hundred foot elevation trail, traverse along a river housed within a large canyon, then make the 3000 foot climb up the steep trail over the rim, and then finally hike along a dirt road back to the campsite. The climb up would be our true test. The younger scouts, however, would do the opposite, climbing down the 3000 foot canyon to meet us in the middle along the banks of the river. We would break for lunch and then separate, my group climbing the difficult trail and the younger scouts hiking the easy path back through the desert.

We used the trail and topographic maps as our guides. The trail on the map seemed to be well marked, though as scouts, we knew that wasn't always the case. We trained for the unexpected, and we knew what to do if we lost the trail. Losing a trail was not a question of if, but when, and knowing what to do when the guides failed could mean the difference between life and death.

The weather was perfect, cool with a light breeze that kept us comfortable in the glow of the eastern rising sun. Plants in full bloom painted the countryside, some with red berries highlighting their bright green leaves. The rocks painted the trail in shades of red, yellow, and orange, adding their own artistic touch to the already colorful landscape. In the west, small white clouds resembling cotton balls dotted the sky above. I watched an eagle catch a wind current and float majestically in circles and wondered if pterodactyls had looked the same when they flew over the Earth. That day, time was not an issue, and we all breathed in the beauty of nature.

The trail headed to where the river exited the canyon, where we would begin the steep ascent. As we neared the river, the sky darkened and the clouds turned from white to gray. I noticed that the foliage around us changed from flowering shrubs to large thorn bushes. Suddenly, I felt a drop of rain. Then another. Then several. The rain fell quickly, coming down in buckets and dampening our gear but not our spirits. As we put our slickers on for the rain, we realized we had ventured off the trail and lost our location. We needed to find our way back to it.

When someone realizes they've lost a trail, they have a few different options. He can choose to continue in his direction, or he can stay put and hope for a rescue. Heading in the same direction may seem like the right thing to do, but oftentimes doing so is a bad idea because one may end up completely confused, or worse. Lost hikers would often die from hypothermia. Officials would find them days or weeks later in a location determined by their delirium.

Second, one can stay where they are and hope for a rescue. Hoping for a rescue is right in certain situations, but is dependent upon several factors of which are beyond the control of the hiker. If the situation is life threatening, waiting for rescue may not always be the best option.

Another option is to trek backwards, follow your tracks, and search for the lost trail. However, there is no telling how far back the trail was lost, and thus the hike could be extended even more. Additionally, it is possible that the trail could be overlooked causing the hiker to get lost once again.

That day we chose none of those options. Instead, we decided to take a risk and cut across the canyon. Then, with the aid of our compasses, we'd search for the trail we'd lost. We had determined the trail was somewhere to our left, in the direct path of the thorn bushes. I looked at the little red berries amidst the thorns, and I decided that they no longer looked inviting.

As we worked our way through the thorns, I noticed my slicker began to tear, and I could feel the rain penetrate the gear as it soaked through my clothes. I looked at Richie's and Kevin's slickers, and I realized that theirs were faring no better. As we moved through the rain and the thorns, I was glad I remembered to bring a second pair of shoes, having learned my lesson the last time we braved Utah.

It took us twenty minutes to get through the thorns, and though our slickers were torn and our clothes were wet, we had found our way back onto the trail. The rain ended and the sun warmed and dried us as we worked our way down to the river. We considered it a small adventure, hiking through the thorns in the rain, but it wasn't anything we couldn't handle. We were proud to find our way back with little damage, all the while hoping we had seen the last of the rain.

With the clouds dissipating and the sun finally shining above, we made our way to the meeting spot at the edge of the river. Off to the east, the river zigzagged between two towering cliffs, marking the entrance to the canyon.

"How high do you think those cliffs are?" asked Jesse.

"They have got to be at least three thousand feet up, because that's what we've got to climb to get out of here," said Josh.

"I hope they don't fall climbing down," said Kevin.

"I hope *we* don't fall climbing up," said Richie.

As we waited for the younger scouts to arrive, we admired our surroundings, and congratulated ourselves on braving the thickets in the rain. We were famished, the adventure taking much of our energy, but we wanted to wait for the others to join us so we could all eat together. We sent two scouts to look into the mouth of the canyon to see if there was any sign of them approaching, but there was no sign. While we sat amongst the cliffs, one of the boys noticed some large animal prints.

"Scoutmaster Chuck," he asked. "Are those prints what I think they are?"

He looked at them and said, "Yes. They look like a mountain lion."

"Maybe lions ate the rest of our troop," said another boy. No one laughed at the joke. It was becoming apparent that the plan we began with was going to have to change.

"What do we do?" I asked. "They have got to come through that canyon. Do we go back the way we came, or do we head into the canyon to meet up with them?"

"We'll probably need to go into the canyon," said Steve.

"We should continue our part of the plan, and if we meet up with them, we'll all stop and rest," said Assistant Scoutmaster Dan.

If we chose to head into the mouth of the canyon, we would stay along our predetermined route and run into the other scouts. At least we hoped. The fact the other scouts had not arrived made some of us wonder if we shouldn't turn back the way we came. The problem with not going forward was that we would leave the younger scouts on their own, and we did not know if they were in any danger or not. We knew we had to go into the mouth of the canyon, and be ready for anything that might come our way.

"Alright then. Let's go," I said. We packed our gear and headed alongside the river. The walls immediately towered above us, and their cliffs blocked the overhead sun. The temperature cooled in the midst of the shadows. The sound of rapids echoed between the cliffs as the icy river traversed amongst the rocks.

Not too long after we entered, we realized we would have to cross the river on more than one occasion. We knew we'd get wet as we crossed the knee-deep water that was ice-cold from the melted Rocky Mountain snow. As we slushed through the water, we realized that the trail was no longer a trail. Instead, the canyon itself became the trail. All we had to do was make our way between the cliffs, and survive.

As the sun moved further west, the clouds above us grew dark. Rain began to fall upon us. We had crossed the river now several times, and water bombarded us from below and above. The air cooled, and our torn slickers were of no use. The younger scouts never appeared, and we felt that something had to have gone drastically wrong. As the sun set, we came to a bank alongside the river that had a slight slope towards the water's edge as it cut into a small embankment. The bank ended three feet above the water. The area was just large enough for us to set up tents so we could get some rest for the night.

Richie and I decided to share a tent. As we hammered our stakes in the ground, I heard Neil ask, "Is that snow?" Sure enough, the rain from above turned into snowflakes. We watched quietly as the flakes drifted slowly to the ground.

"Isn't it June?" asked Josh.

"What kind of weather are we going to see next?" asked Kevin. "It's like we're seeing all four seasons in twenty-four hours."

We cooked our dinners and sat by the small fire, soaking in the limited warmth from its flames. We were worried, exhausted, cold, and wet. Eventually, exhaustion won. The sound of the river continued to echo between the canyon walls as I closed my eyes and fell asleep.

The next morning when I woke up, the ground beneath had shifted. Instead of resting on something solid, the tent felt like a hammock floating in the cool air. I heard the rush of water below me instead of beside me, and realized the tent was not on the ground at all. I was hanging over the embankment inside the tent.

"Richie," I said. "Richie! Don't move. You're keeping me from falling in the water."

"What?" he said sleepily.

"Help me up." I said again.

He looked over and said, "Where are you?" He hadn't yet realized that the stakes did not hold throughout the night, and one wrong move would send both of us into the icy river and the threat of hypothermia.

When Richie realized the situation, he carefully helped me over the bank, and we both scampered out of the tent. We realized how close we were to both going into the river during the night. Gathering our belongings and packing our tent, we ate our oatmeal and mentally prepared to continue our journey. It was cold, and the canyon walls blocked out the sun. Our shoes were wet, and we knew our next layer of clothes would get wet, also. I kept my dry pair of shoes in my backpack. There would be a time to bring them out. The best thing we could do was to continue moving and find our way out of the canyon to the heights above.

We hiked that morning over slippery rocks and waist deep icy cold water. At some point along the route, Russell said, "No wonder we never saw the other scouts. They probably got down here and said, 'Forget this!'"

"If they ever made it down here at all," said Josh. He pointed to the distant sky filled with dark grey clouds. We had no idea whether they carried rain or snow.

Keeping count of how many times we had zigzagged across the river, we hit twenty by the time the sun had passed midday. Tired, worried, and frustrated, we continued our hike, knowing our only option was to press onward. As we walked in silence, we saw two pieces of wood staked into the ground. Beyond the stakes was a thin muddy trail heading up the sides of the cliff. It wound above us in switchbacks, a muddy three-thousand foot escape from the depths of the canyon to the upper ridge above. We stared at the trail, and then each other. A few of the boys gasped at its appearance.

"You've got to be kidding me," said Jesse. "That's our trail?"

The scoutmasters opened the maps and studied them intently. We scanned the sides of the canyon, but we could not find another passage. Two stakes clearly marked this trail. "Is there another way?" asked Kory.

"Doesn't look like it," said Steve.

A steep incline with spots of more than a forty-five degree angle was bad enough, but with the rain and mud, it was very dangerous. I turned back to observe the canyon, and I worried someone could suffer hypothermia if we returned the way we came. It looked like the trail above was our only way out.

"We have no other choice," I said. "But we can make it if we work together."

"Well, up we go," said Dan, and we slowly passed between the two stakes up the muddy trail above.

The climb seemed to take forever. With each full muddy step, we'd slip on the mud, giving up half the ground we gained. Our shoes became heavy with the wet brownish clay. The minutes turned into hours, and in our exhaustion we had no choice but to continue upward. Suddenly, we heard the mechanical thumping of a helicopter. "What are they doing out here?" asked Neil.

"Probably looking for someone who is lost," said Josh.

"Do you think they are looking for the other half of our troop?" asked Kevin.

"Probably not," I said. "I doubt they ever made it down this canyon. They probably took one look at this trail and turned back."

"Maybe they're looking for us," said Kory.

"Could be."

We continued the slow and deliberate steps up the side of the cliff. When we stopped to rest, we looked down behind us and saw the winding river between the canyon walls. Amazed at the distance we'd come, we knew somewhere above the rim would be flat land, and an easier hike back to camp.

Eventually, the switchbacks ended and the ground did level off, signifying the end of our three-thousand foot climb. Exhausted from our ordeal, I breathed a sigh of relief knowing the rest of our journey would be on flatter land. We had hiked in soaking wet clothes and slippery, drenched shoes through the rain, snow, wind, water, and mud. We would take a step forward, only to slide back, increasing our effort and time on the side of the cliff. For young men used to the Las Vegas heat, the June weather in Utah felt more like the blistery winter of January.

We stopped to rest. Through the fog we saw thick fields of alfalfa and clusters of trees scattered across the countryside, an incredible view to behold. My feet were soaked and blistered, so I decided now was the time to change my shoes.

"Wish I had thought of that," said Neil. I smiled wryly.

"So where's the trail?" asked Richie. Surprisingly we noticed for the first time there was no sign of a trail beyond the point where we had just arrived. All we could see was grass.

"That's probably what happened," said Chuck. "They made it to these fields and couldn't find the trail down."

"I bet you're right," said Steve.

"I'm still betting on those mountain lions," someone said.

"So where do we go now?" asked Josh.

We pulled out the maps and compared them to the terrain. By our compass, we knew there would be a road to the east, and if we headed in that direction we'd find it. Picking ourselves up, we trudged eastward across the fields.

The fields were bigger than we expected. We did not have the luxury of a trail, only our compass. We never saw any mountain lions, but we noticed a bull as he ate the wild alfalfa. Standing roughly thirty yards away, he watched us intently as we cautiously walked past.

"Steve," said Josh. "Do you realize there's no fence between us and him?"

"Just keep moving quietly and don't make any aggressive moves," said Steve.

"Is anybody wearing red?" asked Kevin.

"Just keep moving." The bull turned his head to watch us pass while he chewed his alfalfa. Bored with us, he lowered his head and returned to his meal. We all breathed a collective sigh of relief.

A short while later we found the unpaved road. The rain from the night before made it a muddied mess, but it was much easier to navigate than anything we had been through earlier. As the afternoon neared its end, we could see the sun setting through the clouds. The rain had left, and the air had become dry again, evaporating the moisture on our damp clothes. With still no sign of the younger scouts, all we could do was continue to move forward as planned. Double-checking our maps, we headed south along the muddy road, making our way up hill after hill, tired but determined to go as far as we could.

Eventually, the boys had reached their end. I could tell even the scoutmasters were tired. It made sense for everyone to rest and decide on a plan. We decided a small party would leave the rest behind to try to find some help.

Steve and I looked at each other. "I'll continue to go," I said. "I've got dry shoes, so I can make it."

"I can't let you go alone," he said. "I'll come with you." Tired, we said goodbye to the other scouts and began our walk. We walked slowly over a few hills and saw the lake. The road wrapped around the northern edge, and we prepared ourselves to follow the road for as long as necessary. Across the lake, we saw a white truck driving our way leaving a trail of dust behind it.

"Maybe this guy can help us," I said.

As the driver drove nearer, he slowed down and came to a stop next to us. "You must be the lost scouts everyone's looking for," he said.

Steve and I looked at each other. "Nobody told us we were lost," said Steve.

"Well, the entire forest ranger outfit is looking for you."

"Here we are, then. The rest of us are down the road over a couple of hills. We could use some transportation to get back to camp."

"Tell you what," said the driver. "Hop in the back. I'll take you back to camp, and then we'll send help to get the rest."

"Sounds like a plan to me," I said. We climbed aboard and sat down on the floor of the bed of his truck, thankful to rest our legs. As he drove, I gazed upon the sunset off to the west, and I knew my mission to get us back home was nearly complete. Upon our return to camp, a convoy of excited adults got into their vehicles and rushed to pick up the rest of the scouts. I sat on a park bench next to my gear, and Sean rushed over to my side.

"We never found the trail," said Sean. "We got lost around some bull and then the weather hit us. It began to snow several inches, and we had to pitch our tents on some field."

"So you never found the trail down the canyon?" I asked.

"No. We camped in our tents and awoke to a bunch of snow. We didn't know what else to do but to hike back to camp and tell everyone that you were lost."

"We weren't lost," I said. "It sounds like you guys were the ones who were lost."

A few minutes later, the rest of the troop returned. A group of forest rangers asked to see the scoutmasters separately. I watched their faces, and I could tell that our scoutmasters were getting a lecture, though I thought it was undeserved. Our half of the troop knew where we were and, as the situation worsened, we knew exactly what to do. What amazed me was how everybody else seemed to panic. I wondered what had transpired in the fields above while we were in the canyon. Why did they so quickly conclude that we were in danger and in need of assistance, when we had trained and prepared to handle the unexpected?

With everyone safe and accounted for, we headed home, tired, hungry and wet. Upon arrival, I saw my mother waiting for me in her truck. She looked relieved to see me, and I wondered if she was upset.

"Where were you," she asked me.

"In Zion National Park, Mom," I said.

"I know that," she said. "But what did you get into."

"A real adventure," I said.

"Do you know what they told us?"

"No, what?"

"I got a voice message that said, 'The boys are lost in Utah and we're trying to find them. We'll call you when we know more.' Click!"

"I bet you loved hearing that," I said, chuckling, knowing no mother would want to hear such a voice message.

At that moment, Assistant Scoutmaster Dan walked up to her side of the truck. "Mrs. Kunz," he began. "You should be very proud of your son. Having him on that trip was like having another adult."

"Thank you," she said, and my mother beamed with pride. I gave Dan a tired wink and a thumbs-up. We waved goodbye, and drove home.

That night, safe, warm, and most importantly dry in the comfort of my home, I thought about what had happened. I thought of the differences between the two groups of scouts. My group, with the older, more experienced scouts, hiked through the depths of the canyon and made it out again. The younger, less experienced group had panicked. I believed they had done the best they could, but imagined the worst, and thus felt the need to call for assistance.

We had made the mistake of not discussing a contingency plan before separating. We had simply planned to meet in the middle. When the inexperienced scouts above the rim could not find the trail, they returned to camp. They assumed in our absence that we would do the same. We, on the other hand, thought if we did not continue through the canyon, we might miss them, and we were fearful they were lost or needed help. That adventure made me realize how different groups can be in similar situations, yet handle them in completely different ways. Often groups make assumptions that lead to panic, such as the younger scouts had. That panic branched out to our families and worsened.

I learned that people must prepare for all possible outcomes, both positive and negative. We need a clear direction, a contingency plan. If no contingency plan is in place, the plan should be to continue with the original plan, no matter how hard that may be because staying calm and moving forward in all of life's situations is the only way to make it to the top of the peak and see the sunset over the canyon below.

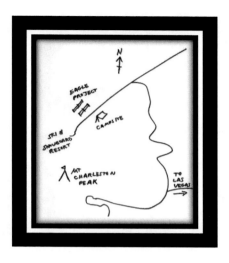

CHAPTER 15
SUCCESSION

SOMETIMES THINGS HAPPEN without even realizing it, and one day we notice that our lives have moved forward, closer to or even reaching a goal. I had spent the last few years checking off boxes for rank advancement, and becoming proficient in skills that led to merit badges. While I focused on our camping trips and my responsibilities as senior patrol leader, I collected additional patches and ranks that brought me closer to the pinnacle of scouting.

I had been a Life Scout for just a year and a half and I had completed my Eagle Project, the fence, long ago. With the fence behind me, I had not felt the urge to sprint to the finish line and become an Eagle. Instead, I had focused on leading my troop. It was more important for me to see their success and advancement than my own, and I thought of that each time I checked off a box.

However, one day I realized there were no more boxes to check, and I had reached that pinnacle of scouting. I felt a hint of sadness.

Elections were coming around the corner, and something inside me told me that it was time to pass the baton to someone else. I had led the troop now for two and a half years. I was unopposed each time I was up for reelection. This time, however, I was going to step down. It was someone else's turn to lead Troop 249.

At the next meeting, I walked to Steve. "Steve, I've got good news," I said.

"Oh? What's that?" I handed him my list with the last item checked off.

"I've done it. I've completed my steps to Eagle," I said.

"That's terrific!" he said, smiling.

"And one more thing," I said. "With elections coming around the corner, I'm not going to run for senior patrol leader again." Steve stared a little bit, but then he quickly had a look of acceptance on his face.

"Ok," he said.

"But I've got a good idea," I continued. "How about we have a camping trip at Mount Charleston, and there we can have a big ceremony for the next senior patrol leader? We haven't done that before, and since it's been so long since anyone else has had the title, we can bring in the new person the right way."

"I like that idea," said Steve.

"I'm going to miss working with you, though. You're a good friend."

"Well, you did a great job, and I appreciate that," said Steve.

We continued the meeting, and I formally announced my decision to leave my position, and a date we would hold our next elections on a camping trip at Mount Charleston. I said they needed to think whether they wanted to run for the position. There were some murmurs from the boys. I had been in front of them for so long that the prospect of seeing someone new in that position was strange.

While some felt sad that I was no longer going to be their leader, others whispered at the prospect of taking the position.

Six weeks later, we were in the Mount Charleston campsite. A few hundred yards away stood the fence we had built so long ago. It stood strong along the hillside amongst the trees. I was quiet on this trip. There was not much to discuss. Many of the boys came to me to thank me for all we had done together. They had questions about attaining the rank of Eagle, and some asked whether I would remain with the troop. I told them what I knew about Eagle, but I could not answer them if I would remain. Something inside me told me to stay quiet.

There was also some question about who was going to take over. I had heard that Josh had some interest, and there were whispers that another boy or two would also consider it. There was no politicking, asking me to support anyone in particular as is often done in adult politics. Instead, there was only the process. I stood back as best I could to let the process complete itself.

As the sun set down behind Charleston's Peak up above, the mountain shadows darkened the woody terrain. We cooked our dinners on the nearby grills provided by the campsite, and we ate joyfully together. The scoutmasters eventually began to put wood in the fire pit, and as the sun disappeared around the earth and the stars above shone their light, the fire lit the area in a dancing orange glow. Everyone gathered around it to get ready for the vote.

Being distant for so long that day, I gathered myself and stood in front of the troop for one last time. "As my last act as senior patrol leader," I began, "I am going to run the process for you to elect your new senior patrol leader. Do we have any nominations?"

"I nominate Josh," said one boy. I looked at Josh, and he sat there quietly looking at me. He was an older scout, and had been with the troop since before I was involved. He was nearing Eagle, but had never held the highest position. As I looked at him, I thought of all the experiences we shared together.

"Ok," I said. "Do we have any others?" A few quiet seconds went by, but nobody said anything. "Are we sure we have no other nominations?" I asked again. There were only the crickets chirping from the nearby bushes. "Ok, then. We may not need an election. We can probably do this by a show of hands, unless," and I looked at Josh, "Josh, would you like to say a few words before the vote?"

"Josh shook his head and said, "I'll wait until after."

"Alright," I continued. "All in favor of Josh being your new senior patrol leader, please raise your hands and say 'Aye!'" The troop all raised their hands in approval of Josh. I looked at him. It occurred to me that I never actually sat down with Josh to tell him all I knew about what it took to run a troop. He had been in leadership positions as a patrol leader for a long time, and I was sure he had his own ideas. I had hoped that he had been watching me, learning all the things I did right, as well as all the many things I did wrong. Still, I was bothered that my time was ending and that I never helped fully prepare him. I worried how that would affect the troop.

"With that being said, my last act as senior patrol leader is to congratulate the new senior patrol leader of Troop 249, Josh!" I looked at Josh and said, "Come on up here and say a few words to your troop." Josh stood and began his speech. I heard him say that the goal of reaching Philmont was on his mind, and that pleased me. While he was talking, I stepped behind the boys, away from the fire pit, and into the shadows. It was Josh's troop now, and I knew the best thing for the troop was for me to disappear.

I watched them in the orange glow from a distance. Would they be ready? Will they succeed? Did I do everything I knew to do? Could I have done more? Should I have done less? I said a quiet prayer for Josh and the troop, nervous at the right of passage each of us would undertake.

With the Eagle process now complete, I knew it would not be long before I would move on to different challenges, leaving my friends in the troop to experience new adventures of their own.

CHAPTER 16
THE QUESTION

DRESSED IN FULL UNIFORM, my sash proudly displaying thirty-three merit badges, I sat, nervous, across from the local area council, waiting to begin the last step in the approval process to becoming an Eagle Scout. Each of the three representatives would interview me before they would accept me into the elite group of scouts.

I anticipated their possible questions, knowing one question in particular could create conflict. Would they ask it, I wondered? Would they deny the award to me if my answer were not satisfactory? I thought of the first line of the Scout Law, "A Scout is Trustworthy…" If they asked me the question, I would tell them the truth. What they would then choose to do would be up to them, not me.

In the scouts, becoming an Eagle was an important event, and involved planning from more than just the family and the troop. The troop council had already approved me, and notifications had been prepared to send to members of the Nevada United States Senate and House of Representatives. The scoutmasters discussed with my family how to order awards and invitations for my Eagle Court of Honor. Even with all of that in progress, I still had to make it through the final interview, and the one question I knew they'd ask. It would be a shame if, after all of our efforts, I told them the truth and I was not approved.

The interview began.

"I see you're wearing a polar bear patch from a long time ago," one representative asked. He was referring to the patch I earned by spending several minutes over three separate days in an ice-cold pool in the Arizona mountains. Remembering the experience, I could almost feel the freezing water covering my. "Why haven't you changed that patch to a more recent one?"

I did not need to consider my answer carefully. "Over the years, I collected a lot of patches that could rightly replace it, but I've kept it since I earned it during my first summer camp in Arizona to remind myself to never do that again." I smiled and said, "That was one of the coldest experiences of my life, and I'm proud to have said, 'I did it.' I thought I'd be asked to do it again and, honestly, I didn't want to so I figured wearing it would stop people from asking. It worked like a charm." The three of them chuckled and it seemed to lighten the mood.

The second question came from one of the other representatives. "Which merit badge was the hardest for you to earn?"

"Well, unfortunately I earned a reputation for being a bad cook after my experience of burning oatmeal at Keyhole Canyon."

"How does one burn oatmeal?" she asked.

"Exactly my point!" I said. "I have no idea how I did it, but it happened, and I had to scrape off the burned oatmeal from the bottom of the pot with a rock. It took forever, so I had this reputation and it became sort of a victory celebration for the entire troop for me to earn my cooking merit badge."

She laughed. "Did they let you cook for them after you earned the merit badge?"

"Not at all," I said. "I handled the kitchen cleaning for every meal during every camping trip, unless it was assigned to someone else. Our scoutmasters taught us to determine who did what best and let them do it. It was obvious cooking wasn't something I did well at all, but I did get the merit badge."

"I see you were a Life Scout for a long time. Why'd it take you so long to get your Eagle?"

"I never really focused on myself, because I guess I never felt it was about me," I said. I took a long breath and continued, "I was the senior patrol leader for two and a half years and I felt during that time it was my job to lead the boys in my troop, not be concerned with my own rank advancement."

"Can you provide an example of how you did that?" she asked.

"Yes, for the last few years I've been preparing them to tackle Mount Baldy at Camp Philmont. It's funny, but I've been more concerned with their experiences and their rank advancement than my own, but I honestly hadn't thought of it that way. I just knew it was important for the troop as a whole to grow."

The man on the left, quiet most of the time finally spoke. "Matt, are you planning on staying in the scouts once you become an Eagle?"

I closed my eyes and exhaled, for he had asked me the anticipated question. At almost sixteen, I would have two more years of eligibility, and they wanted to know if I would stay involved. From their vantage point, my staying in the scouts would be an example for younger scouts to achieve their Eagle. My thoughts wrestled between their desire for me to stay and another desire welling up inside me.

As I considered my answer, all the memories and lessons flooded my thoughts, followed closely by adventures I imagined considering outside of scouts, the things I wanted to do to make a difference in the world.

"I've been in a leadership role since my second week in the scouts," I began. "During all that time, I've seen a great group of people trying to find a way to work together for the troop in what can be a crazy world. I've seen lives get saved and I've climbed the top of mountains. I've seen how corruption can hurt an organization, and I've faced a rowdy audience head on. I've been lost or stranded in and around Utah on two separate occasions. I've learned that challenges we can't explain come our way, only to find out later that often times we are the cause of them. Being a scout has helped me gain a lot of wisdom, but I feel like I need to use these experiences in other areas. My school needs peer leaders, and I feel like that's something I should do. I have to work over the summers now, and my sports are more demanding than before. Since I am interested in playing sports in college, I feel like I've got a lot on my plate, and I'm worried I won't be successful if I don't have balance. But we know that once a scout achieves the rank of Eagle, he's always an Eagle Scout, and I know that whatever I'm doing, I'll do it in a way that honors that rank. And along with that, I will always owe my time in the scouts and Troop 249 a ton of gratitude." I did not think my answer was the one they wanted, but I hoped they understood and appreciated my honesty. They asked a few more questions and, without giving me their decision, finished the interview.

I waited patiently several long days until I received a call from Scoutmaster Steve. "Congratulations," he said. "You've been approved! Now we need to figure out what to do for your ceremony."

"What are you thinking?" I asked.

"How about a roast!"

Feeling embarrassed for the need for ceremony, I knew the events were as much a thank you to the boys in my troop as much as it was an awards ceremony for me. I hoped it would be an inspiration for them to strive to achieve their own rank of Eagle.

On the night of the event, the entire troop dressed in uniform, I stood next to Scoutmaster Steve as he spoke to the group about the adventures and the fun we shared. I looked at Scoutmasters Chuck and Dan, and Richie and all the boys. They laughed at my refusal to remove my Polar Bear patch, and gave me a hard time for always finding a way to send over the biggest, dirtiest vehicles during our carwash fundraisers. We shared memories of chasing chickens down the abandoned mineshaft, and they wondered how it was possible to burn oatmeal. We remembered the emergency drill on Mount Potosi and counted the number of new scouts we sent on so many prank snipe hunts. I thought of the peach cobbler we ate around our many campfires, all the places we had been, the stories we told, and the memories we shared.

We remembered the funny and unusual things, and though we never discussed the lessons mentioned in this book, I knew that, like me, they sat in the back of each of our minds. I understood, then, the reason for our ceremonies. They were to celebrate and honor each other, to be thankful for our mutual experiences and appreciate our time together. I was honored to be in the presence of my friends, and grateful that the ceremony had not been about me, but had instead been a stroll down memory lane, a collective appreciation of our shared experiences. I would not have wanted it any other way.

When the celebration ended and I stepped out of my church, I admired the beauty of the sun slowly setting to the west, just making its way below Mount Charleston and sending red and orange hues across the Las Vegas Valley. My parents headed to the car, but I stood and watched the sun dip behind the mountain, remembering when I'd signed my name in the journal that day on top of the summit, and it was then that I understood I'd climbed another peak that night and accomplished something that would remain with me forever.

CHAPTER 17
ONE LAST VISIT

I HAD BEEN AWAY FROM TROOP 249 for over a year. Sports and honors courses had become more demanding, and life was busy, but I had missed the troop and decided to take the time to just stop by and say hello. When I arrived, I saw that there was new construction and a new location for the boys to hold their meetings. Unannounced, I opened the doors to their meeting to surprise them.

I heard my name called from behind me. I turned and saw Sean running in my direction. He still looked like he had in the past, and I chuckled that, yet again, Sean was running.

"Hi, Sean! How've you been?"

"Good! We made it to Philmont!"

"You did? How was it?"

"It was awesome! You should have come."

"Sounds great, and I'm sure it was. I couldn't come with you, but I'm so glad you made it."

As I looked at the boys, Sean was the only one I recognized. Everyone else was new, their faces showing excitement for scouting adventures of their own. I assumed the other boys, like me, transitioned their time to other areas of their lives. However, another friend remained. Towering over them all was Scoutmaster Steve. I went up to say hello.

"You came back!" said Steve in his deep voice.

"Well, I missed you guys, and I wanted to come and see how things have been," I said.

"It's a whole new troop," said Steve. "Well, except Sean. He's one of the older boys now."

"Where's everyone else?"

"They all earned their Eagles and moved on," said Steve. "A few managed to achieve their Eagle right at the last minute, but they made it."

"I'm so glad to hear it."

"I'm glad you're here," he said. "We just had elections and we have a new senior patrol leader. He may need some pointers. Do you have a minute?"

Steve called over a very young scout. He was smaller in stature, and I could tell by his rank that he hadn't been a scout for long. Yet, he was elected and was now in charge of his troop. I wondered if I was this young when I first offered to lead, and it occurred to me that I was. I could tell by the look on his face that he took his position seriously, but he still had a lot to learn.

After a quick introduction, I asked him if he had any questions.

"Well, I do have one question," he said.

"What's that?"

"Why won't they listen to me?" I smiled thinking of all the times I had asked that question myself due to the frustration I sometimes felt. The young scout had no idea just how common his question was among leaders.

"Leadership doesn't just come with a title," I said. "It has to be earned every single day. You don't do that by telling them what to do. You do that by inspiring them to be their best."

"Well, how do I do that?" he asked. I thought back to those first few weeks when I had joined the scouts, how I had read a book on how to be a patrol leader, and how we changed our name to the Gator Patrol and made our flag. I thought about how we took on challenges above and beyond what others would accept, and how, even in the midst of turmoil, we hung together.

"You'll have to find your own voice, and come up with your own ideas," I said. "But whatever you do, do it for them. Just remember that it's not about you."

It was apparent he did not quite get what I had said, and I knew he would experience baptism by fire until he learned for himself the lessons I had learned. Steve and I talked some more and said our farewells. As I drove away, I was happy that I made the visit, and I smiled when I imagined Sean running up the peaks of Philmont.

The Scout Oath

On my honor I will
do my best to do
my duty to God and
my Country and to obey
the Scout Law. To help
other people at all times,
to keep myself physically
strong, mentally awake,
and morally straight.

CONCLUSION

OVER THE NEXT SEVERAL YEARS, I took on new challenges and experienced new adventures. I captained two varsity sports in high school, and won the award for "Most Outstanding Senior Young Man" from my graduating class.

I played football as a walk-on for the University of Notre Dame, and used many of the leadership skills I had learned as a scout to deal with the high pressure and politics of the sport. I credit my ability to speak in front of a crowd to my time as senior patrol leader for it prepared me for a pep rally talk that ultimately led to my first post-college job.

Eventually I met a wonderful woman. When I proposed I was thrilled she accepted. Though I have not spoken with her about these experiences much, there have been times during our travels when I've mentioned being stranded in Arizona, or the search for the troop in Utah.

I have told her stories about the Troop 249 members and leaders, about Jeff, Chuck, Richie, Steve, Neil, Robbie, Kory, Dan, Russell, Jesse, Kevin, Josh, Sean, and all the boys. She has learned the importance of that time in my life as I have shared my memories buried from years gone by. She has since understood the importance of being a scout, and achieving the rank of Eagle. Once she came upon a group of scouts selling popcorn outside the grocery store.

"My husband was once an Eagle Scout," she told them.

"Ma'am," one scout said. "Once you're an Eagle Scout, you're *always* an Eagle Scout." My wife was impressed with the young man's conviction. I smiled at the thought of him speaking of the award so honorably, and I would not doubt if his conviction had led him to achieve the award himself.

On a trip back to Las Vegas, while attending Mass with my family, I noticed an assistant priest off to the side. I knew that gangly, tall figure immediately. It was my Scoutmaster, Steve.

I had not seen him in over ten years, but as I watched him proudly assist with Mass, it was as if no time had passed, and I thought back to the time he confided in me all those years before. I remembered that trip down the Colorado River when we ran from the lightning, and he'd shared how he felt he was being called to the Priesthood, and I saw that, after all this time, God's purpose had been fulfilled.

Years later, I would have other challenges that would come my way. I would experience many successes and failures. Some of these lessons I would have to painfully relearn, but when I took my seat on the Milton City Council on a January night, I thought back to the boys of Troop 249 and the lessons we learned. I knew we would have many challenges that would come before us, but we could find a way. Though the world could be crazy, we could make it through so long as we did our best to work together.

At the end of each day, I would go out of my way to find the sunset. As I'd watch the sky turn from orange to red and purple hues

I'd think about the nature I experienced out west, and I would ask myself if I *did my best, to do my duty, to God and my country.* Every now and again, I would see an eagle soar quietly in the sky. During those quiet moments, I would know that it is time to rest, for there would be another mountain to climb with my friends tomorrow.

TO THE READER

THANK YOU FOR READING! I hope you enjoyed *To God and My Country*. I have to tell you, this was an extremely emotional book. As I wrote it, I remembered all these lessons, the friends I made, and the challenges we overcame. So many experiences later in my life were successful due to these stories, and I was both humbled and overjoyed being able to share each one.

My hope is that this book will be an inspiration as you remember similar times, find yourself in the middle of an adventure, or plan an exploration beyond a great horizon. Whatever your compass direction, let these stories be a guide into human nature. Remember that in the end there is no joy in success without friends to celebrate with you.

Finally, I need to ask a favor. If you would, please write a review of *To God and My Country*. Whether you loved it or hated it, I would appreciate your feedback.

Reviews can be tough to come by these days. You, the reader, have the power to make or break a book. If you have the time, please write a review on Amazon.com, Barnesandnoble.com, Goodreads.com, or any other online book retailer website.

Thank you again for enjoying *To God and My Country*, and may you too soar like an Eagle!

ACKNOWLEDGEMENTS

THERE ARE MANY TO THANK for the creation of this book, as writing a memoir about a time with very important people and memories can be extremely emotional. First, I have to thank God, whose creation of nature and safekeeping during adventure allowed me to have these experiences.

Secondly, thank you to my wife, RaDonna, for encouraging me to write about this time in my life when I doubted whether I should.

Thank you to my mother, Mary Sue, and my father, George, for sharing my idea with others and for relaying how so many thought that a message of this sort would be valuable.

Thank you to the Boy Scouts of America, and the programs they instilled during my time with them. Thank you to all my scoutmasters and assistant scoutmasters, both those I mentioned and those I did not. It's tough to tell every story when writing a book, but my memories of each of you helped make me who I am today.

Finally, thank you to the boys of Troop 249. I think of you far more often than you'll ever know. Each time I remember you it always leads me to smile, and it inspires me to look towards the horizon for another adventure.

ABOUT THE AUTHOR

BUSINESS MAN, CITY COUNCILMAN, volunteer, coach, Eagle Scout, and former football player, Matt Kunz understands what it takes to win on and off the field. A former walk-on linebacker and special-teams player for the Fighting Irish of Notre Dame, he holds a Bachelor of Arts degree in American Studies.

Through his experiences, Matt learned valuable lessons about leadership, politics, and coaching. Not only was he a football coach for several seasons, but he became a City Councilman in the City of Milton and has been working on initiatives to help maintain the rural and equestrian spirit. He also spent three years as the President of the Friends of the Milton Library, helping lead a team to build the Milton Library and the barn bookstore, made from wood from local barns.

His business, government, and volunteer activities have made a difference in his community. He attributes his service mentality to his Catholic faith and his time with Troop 249.

Matt, his wife RaDonna, and their family dogs, live in Milton, Georgia. A frequent speaker, Matt motivates and encourages individuals to be the best they can be on and off the field.

Follow Matt on Twitter at **@MattKunz59**, on his author page at **www.facebook.com/mattkunzauthor**, or on his blog at **https://mattkunz59.wordpress.com**

ALSO BY MATT KUNZ

Triumph! An Athletes Guide to Winning On and Off the Field

"Coaches, you're going to want to give a copy of *Triumph!* to every one of your players. It will not only help them compete at a higher level, but it will also make you a better coach!"
– **Coach Ted Marchibroda**, NFL Head Coach Baltimore Colts 1975 – 1979, Indianapolis Colts 1992 – 1995, Baltimore Ravens 1996 – 1998

"Good teams all do the same things to prepare, yet the intangibles are what determine whether they become great. *Triumph!* addresses all those intangibles and will truly prepare you to be a champion both on and off the field!"
—**Coach Tim McFarlin**, 34-year Georgia High School football coach at Roswell HS and Blessed Trinity HS, 2006 State Champion,

"The lessons I learned from Coach Matt on the football field I carry to this day with me in my everyday life. For example, if the ball doesn't bounce your way, that's when you find out what you're made of. Not everything in life will be in your favor, but how you handle yourself in the face of adversity is all that matters. As you read through *Triumph!,* soak it all in. It will make you a champion in more ways than one."
—**Ali Rezvan**, University of Georgia student, economics major, former, President of Alpharetta HS Future Business Leaders of America